D1305852

scandinavian living

scandinavian living

Magnus Englund & Chrystina Schmidt

photography by Andrew Wood

RYLAND
PETERS
& SMALL

LONDON NEW YORK

First published in the United States in 2003 by
Ryland Peters & Small, Inc.
519 Broadway
5th Floor
New York NY 10012
www.rylandpeters.com

10 9 8 7 6 5 4 3 2 1

Text copyright © Magnus Englund 2003
Design and photographs copyright
© Ryland Peters & Small 2003

All rights reserved. No part of this publication may
be reproduced, stored in a retrieval system, or
transmitted in any form or by any means, electronic,
mechanical, photocopying, recording, or otherwise,
without the prior permission of the publisher.

ISBN 1 84172 412 2

Library of Congress Cataloging-in-Publication Data

Englund, Magnus.
  Scandinavian style / Magnus Englund & Chrystina
Schmidt ; photography by Andrew Wood.
      p. cm.
Includes index.
  ISBN 1-84172-412-2
  1. Design--Scandinavia--History--20th century. 2.
Interior decoration--Scandinavia--History--20th
century. I. Schmidt, Chrystina.
II. Wood, Andrew. III. Title.

NK1457.A1 E54 2003
747'.0948--dc21

                        2002013056

Printed and bound in China

SENIOR DESIGNER Paul Tilby
SENIOR EDITOR Annabel Morgan
LOCATION RESEARCH Chrystina Schmidt
  and Claire Hector
PRODUCTION Deborah Wehner
ART DIRECTOR Gabriella Le Grazie
PUBLISHING DIRECTOR Alison Starling

contents

introduction

Scandinavian modern design, as a style, first emerged between World Wars I and II, but peaked in popularity in the 1950s and is in back in vogue again today. It includes objects designed in Denmark, Finland, Iceland, Norway, and Sweden. Scandinavia is the geographical region around Scandia, the mountain ridge running along Norway and Sweden, a land mass that included Denmark before the Ice Age separated Denmark from the north. Most Scandinavians refer to this area as the Nordic region, rather than Scandinavia.

Until the end of the 19th century, the Nordic region was a poor agricultural backwater. For most Scandinavians, money was short, and eking a living from the land was a struggle. As a result, homes and possessions were simple, spare, and functional. This pared-down design ethos continued into the industrial era, which started later in Scandinavia than in the rest of western Europe. Decorative objects were produced mainly for the small upper class, and were often based on patterns borrowed from France, Germany, and Britain.

During the 1920s a new decorative style appeared in Sweden, an elegant combination of modern lines and simple yet traditional detailing that appealed to the developing middle class. The new style received international recognition, and was labeled Swedish Grace. However, it was soon superseded by something altogether more radical. Also in the 1920s, young Scandinavian architects were amazed and excited by the

left **Closeness to nature is a recurring theme in Scandinavian architecture. Buildings often blend into the surrounding landscape, but sometimes the contrast between modern architecture and nature can be dramatic.**

opposite **All the Scandinavian countries have long coastlines and a multitude of lakes. The winters might be cold and dark, but the summers are warm and bright and the summer nights are long, encouraging relaxed alfresco living.**

modernist style emerging in Germany and France, which was replacing decorative detailing with designs based purely on function and modern technology. When the Swedish architect Gunnar Asplund designed the Stockholm Exhibition of 1930, he turned it into a manifesto for the new style. The exhibition sent a shock wave through the Nordic countries and established modernism (or functionalism, as it was often referred to in northern Europe) as the order of the future.

From the 1930s on, the Social Democrats dominated political life in Scandinavia and put into place a tax-funded welfare state program. Housing, schools, libraries, and hospitals were built at a rapid rate, giving Scandinavian architects and designers new opportunities. The design and layout of new houses, in particular kitchens and bathrooms, were standardized to improve function and hygiene. The design of household

this page Organic shapes and styles are characteristic of Scandinavian design, and reached a peak during the 1950s. These fluid, curvaceous outlines were very different to the modern designs of the Bauhaus designers, which employed square shapes and hard lines, but Scandinavian designers still remained true to the idea of creating simple, functional forms.

left Quality of light is naturally a priority in a region where the sun sets in early afternoon during the winter months. The arrival of electric light opened up new possibilities and spurred designers on to create the ultimate light source for reading, eating, and working.

right and below Fine carving and polishing of wood is a heritage that all the Scandinavian countries share. The old farming culture survived in Scandinavia longer than in most of western Europe, and making houses, furniture, and tools from wood was part of daily life. Furniture and other pieces by master woodturners and cabinetmakers point to this heritage.

items, such as ovens, tableware, and door hardware, was reassessed to improve quality and performance. The 1930s also saw modern Scandinavian design making a breakthrough on the international stage. The Finnish architect Alvar Aalto exhibited his furniture at Fortnum & Mason in London in 1933 and at the Museum of Modern Art (MoMA) in New York in 1938. He also designed the Finnish pavilion at the New York World Fair of 1939. The Swedish designer Bruno Mathsson's furniture was selected for the MoMA collection before the museum even opened. Meanwhile, the Danish company Louis Poulsen enjoyed tremendous success with Poul Henningsen's PH lamps.

After years of rationing during World War II, there was an enormous demand for consumer goods in the Scandinavian home market. Production was fueled by a desperate need for export revenue to kick-start the Nordic economies again, particularly in Finland, which had to pay off a large war debt to the Soviet Union. While Europe remained war-torn and economically crippled, the Americans adopted Scandinavian design as the style of preference for a new, modern age. The prestigious Georg Jensen store on Fifth Avenue was a center for Scandinavian design in the United States. When the new United Nations headquarters was built in Manhattan, Scandinavian designers were responsible for much of the interior. Meanwhile, Scandinavian designers were also winning prestigious awards at exhibitions across the world.

During the late 1960s, a divide between industrial designers and designers as artists became apparent in Scandinavia. The focus on individual designers and their products was questioned by a new, more politically aware generation. What had happened to the idealistic notion of creating good design for everyone? Scandinavian industrial design remained successful, but decorative design began to fall into decline. Italy continued to turn out a large number of innovative and exciting products, beside which Scandinavian designs looked dated and predictable. Glassworks, ceramic factories, and textile companies faced dramatically falling sales, and many went out of business. For the manufacturers who remained, the only option was to follow foreign trends, often with depressing and unsuccessful results.

It was not until the late 1980s that a talented new generation of designers emerged in Sweden. Names such as Thomas Eriksson, Pia Wallén, Björn Dahlström, and Thomas Sandell began to receive international attention, and leading Italian manufacturers such as Cappellini invited Swedish designers to work for them. The result was an explosion of creativity that has put Scandinavia firmly back on the design map. This rediscovery of a regional design identity is evident in all the Scandinavian countries and has certainly been assisted by the international revival of interest in mid-20th-century design classics, which to a large degree focuses on Scandinavian design.

above The warm and relaxed mix of different styles, materials, and colors in Scandinavian homes is far removed from the usual perception of a pared-down and minimalist Scandinavian interior. Wooden floors are always preferred, both in flats and houses, and timber production is a major industry.

right To combine old and new often makes an interior more personal. But Scandinavian kitchens are seldom anything but modern throughout, and function as the engine room of the home. There is a strong focus on developing new productions for the domestic kitchen, be it glassware, flatware, or other utensils, which makes Scandinavian design companies working in this field an international force.

this page Making the most of the available light is achieved with large windows, but the Scandinavian climate also calls for good insulation and effective heating. There are few houses that do not have double glazing, and many have triple glazing to conserve energy and the environment while saving heating costs. The practical, ethical, and economical often come together in Scandinavian design.

elements

WOOD

Wood has always played a starring role in Scandinavian design. Each country has its own favorite: the Danes use beech and the Swedes pine, while the Finns prefer birch.

Historically, buildings, furniture, tools, and household utensils in Scandinavia were to a large degree crafted from wood. While plastic, steel, and concrete briefly stole the show during the 1970s and 1980s, wood has now resumed center stage in Scandinavian design and architecture, often in unusual or unexpected ways. The new Nordic Embassy complex in Berlin is a good example of the use of wood in contemporary architecture.

above Dense Finnish pine and birch forests surround a house built from the same woods. The façade is made from pine while the interior floors and ceilings are crafted from birch.

right The stairwell of Jyrki Tasa's house in Finland is clad with birch veneer. In undiluted functionalist thinking, the construction is true to its purpose: what you see is what there is.

Before the advent of mobile phones, timber production was the dominant industry in Finland, and wood remains close to the heart of Finnish culture and the Finnish people. Wood has always been a major influence on Finnish design, architecture, and interiors, and continues to be so today. A quarter of all Finns have summer houses, and few of these are without wooden saunas. The multitalented Finnish designer Tapio Wirkkala is perhaps best known for his work in glass, but he was a prolific designer in many other materials, including wood. His sculptural pieces created from layered laminated wood and his exquisite wooden tables and bowls were directly influenced by the

opposite above **These veneered tables by Tapio Wirkkala are a perfect example of his awareness of the decorative potential of pure wood.**

opposite below **A soaped oak sideboard designed by Eva Lilja Löwenhielm and Anya Sebton.**

left **The arrival of the wood-veneer Series 7 chair in 1955 set a new standard for mass-produced furniture. This sideboard and table are also made from wood veneer. Like many town houses in Scandinavia, this one has hand-laid parquet flooring.**

below **Mixed with cotton, wood fibers can be spun into fabric and used for a multitude of products, like these seating cubes and cushions by Woodnotes.**

right **The Finnish textile designer Ritva Puotila has worked with wood fibers since the early 1960s, and her large-scale artworks can be found in many Finnish homes, institutions, and corporate buildings.**

Wood functions well as an insulator against cold. During World War II, the Finns used spun wood fibers as a replacement for cotton.

densely forested Finnish landscape. Wirkkala's work in glass, steel, ceramic, and plastic was also influenced by nature, and the elements and many of his designs were first made as prototypes in wood.

Wood has a unique density and functions well as an insulator against cold. During World War II, the Finns used spun wood fibers as a replacement for cotton. Products such as blinds, rugs, and upholstery textiles can all be fashioned from spun wood fibers mixed with cotton. The Finnish designer Ritva Puotila has been a pioneer in this field. During the last thirty years, she has created both spectacular art pieces and more practical household products from humble wood fibers for her company, Woodnotes.

When Alvar Aalto first encountered the tubular-steel furniture of the Bauhaus in the late 1920s, his reaction was to adapt the Bauhaus design principles to a manufacturing process that better fitted both the Finnish tradition and his own idea of functional furniture. Aalto's main challenge was to find a way of bending wood in the same way

This page Aalto furniture is still manufactured using a technique that was originally developed in the early 1930s. Pieces are made from a single piece of birch wood that has been sliced lengthwise, then glued back together, locked in position, steamed, and bent.

above and right Alvar Aalto designed the Paimio chair in 1931–2 for a sanatorium in the Finnish village of Paimio. While comfortable, it forces the sitter to sit upright, thereby improving breathing. The holes in the back are to relieve the tension created by bending the wood—the same problem Arne Jacobsen encountered when designing his Ant chair.

ALVAR AALTO 100 1898 1998

artek

that the Bauhaus architects and designers bent steel. After much experimentation, Aalto developed a new technique using steam and heat to bend and mold wood—a technique that is still in use today. For Aalto, wood represented a more humane, sympathetic material for a better, more democratic world—it was a warm yet practical material suitable for use in hospitals, schools, and kindergartens. His choice of wood as a material can be seen as a political statement, not just a functional choice.

At the same time as Aalto was experimenting with bending and molding wood, the Swedish designer Bruno Mathsson was designing chairs using similar techniques, but with a very different end result. Mathsson came from a long line of cabinetmakers and devoted his long career (from the 1930s to the 1980s) to designing chairs that aimed to maximize the sitter's comfort. Mathsson was a bold innovator who devoted much time to the study of how people actually sat, years before the word ergonomic was in common usage. Mathsson's furniture designs were a huge sales success and made him the most well-known and respected Swedish furniture designer of the twentieth century.

When the world went wild about plastic in the 1950s, Scandinavian countries still continued to produce a huge number of wooden objects. Teak was the wood of choice, particularly in Denmark, for furniture and housewares, including items such as salad servers, ice buckets, trays, sculptures, toys, and much more. The long tradition of fine cabinetmaking remained strong in Denmark, and these traditional skills were

left Børge Mogensen's Spanish chair is one of his most characteristic designs. It was inspired by traditional Spanish furniture designs, which Mogensen was introduced to by Kaare Klint, his tutor at the Royal Academy of Fine Arts.

below left An easy chair model no. 2254 by Børge Mogensen from 1958, upholstered in fabric designed by Lis Ahlmann. The seat of the chair slides forward to allow the back to recline.

above right During the 1950s, Denmark produced a huge amount of high-quality and sophisticated domestic items fashioned from teak and other dark woods. This ice bucket was designed by Finn Juhl.

below right Between 1951 and 1954, Finn Juhl designed a series of wooden bowls for Kay Bojesen, a silversmith now most famous for his wooden monkey, which has become something of a national symbol in Denmark.

opposite, above left Finn Juhl was a master of detail. His most intricate furniture, such as this chair from 1946, was built in collaboration with master cabinetmaker Niels Vodder.

opposite, below left and right Side tables and cocktail trolleys were very much in vogue during the 1950s and '60s. On top of an Alvar Aalto trolley model no. 901 (left) sits an ice bucket from 1960 designed by Jens Quistgaard and manufactured by Dansk International. Dansk was an American company set up in the 1950s to produce and market Danish designs in the U.S. and Europe.

opposite, far right These bowls are made from teak, which has unique qualities. It is heavy and dense, making it hard to work with, but it can withstand moisture like few other woods. Wild teak is endangered, but it can be obtained from approved producers.

The ingenious use of different woods and various skilled joining techniques means that many Danish pieces from this era are works of art.

combined with contemporary styles, resulting in high-quality hand-made Danish wood furniture that was was hugely successful in the 1950s. Designers such as Kaare Klint, Finn Juhl, and Hans Wegner designed chairs that won awards around the world and made Danish furniture into a major industry. The ingenious use of different woods and various skilled joining techniques used in the manufacturing process means that many Danish pieces from this era are works of art. Hans Wegner claimed that if a chair is still beautiful when turned upside down, then it is a good chair, and he applied this conviction to some 500 different designs. Many designs are still made today in small workshops across Denmark, some by the very same craftsmen who first made them half a century ago.

left The PK 0 chair by Poul Kjaerholm from 1952 is an unusual experiment in bent wood by a designer best known for working in steel, glass, and marble. It was not put into production until 1997, when Fritz Hansen produced 600 numbered chairs.

right Arne Jacobsen's Series 7 chair is the single most recognizable piece of Scandinavian design. Since its introduction, copies have flooded the market, including the one used as a prop in the famous photograph of Christine Keeler. The main difference between copies and originals lies in the quality of construction. Fritz Hansen, the original manufacturer, uses cotton sheets interlined between layers of laminate, which gives greater flexibility to the shell.

opposite The Wishbone Chair (known as the Y chair in Scandinavia) by Hans Wegner, dating from 1955, is his bestselling design. To this day, each individual chair is still signed by the craftsman who made it.

During the 1940s, the American aeronautical engineering industry developed a new method of bending and molding plywood. The technique was soon applied to furniture design by the innovative American designers Charles and Ray Eames. In 1952, the Danish architect and designer Arne Jacobsen developed a stackable chair made from a single piece of plywood on a tubular steel base that was suitable for mass production. Jacobsen's biggest difficulty was eliminating the tension in the wood. As a result, he designed a chair with a very narrow waist, roughly resembling the shape of an ant.

Jacobsen approached the established Danish furniture manufacturer Fritz Hansen, with whom he had previously worked, but they were cautious about committing themselves to the production of this strange new design. To get the project off the ground, Jacobsen placed an order for 300 chairs for the

architectural project he was currently working on, convincing Fritz Hansen that it was worth investing in the necessary equipment to produce the chair. In 1955 another Jacobsen plywood chair, the Series 7, was launched. With a broader back and four steel legs, it offered increased comfort and stability, and soon became a standard for all stackable plywood tubular-steel-legged chairs. Available today in beech, ash, cherry, and walnut as well as dozens of lacquered colors, this chair remains the single most recognizable piece of modern Scandinavian furniture design.

left This unique series of vases, named Kivi (Stone) for obvious reasons, were designed by Ritva Puotila at Hadeland glass works in Norway in 1989. She was working as an experimental glass designer and freelance designer for Hadeland at the time. Today the vases are on display in the home of her son, Mikko Puotila.

this picture Ann Wåhlström works for Kosta Boda in Sweden and bridges the gap between the studio glass tradition and the heritage of Swedish glassmaking. On the left is a Soap Bubble vase, and on the right a vase that represents a unique experiment with colors.

opposite above The PK 61 table by Poul Kjærholm has as its top a thick piece of toughened glass that reveals the intricate construction of the asymmetrically positioned steel legs.

GLASS

The concept of art glass is relatively new to Scandinavian countries, where most of the important glassworks were still producing bottle and window glass up until the 1920s.

The starting point for the modern Scandinavian glass industry was the international success of the Swedish glassworks Orrefors, founded in 1898. With the arrival of the artists Simon Gate in 1917 and Edward Hald in 1918, a new era dawned at Orrefors. New techniques and styles were developed, and Orrefors won numerous awards at the Paris fair of 1925 for its Swedish Grace-style vases. Orrefors' success continued up to and through the 1950s with designers like Ingeborg Lundin and Sven Palmqvist and with Gunnar Cyrén in the 1960s. Like so many other Scandinavian glassworks, Orrefors suffered a decline in the 1970s, but today they have some strong new designers, including Ingegerd Råman and Lena Bergström.

Traditionally, Orrefors' main competitor was Kosta Boda, founded in 1742 and named after the two glassworks Kosta and Boda.

Finnish glass is very different from Swedish—less inviting and flirtatious, perhaps, but just as advanced and refined. Perhaps the best-known glass object in the world is the Savoy vase, designed by Alvar Aalto in 1936 and produced by the Finnish glassworks Iittala in the remote Finnish village of the same name.

Today Orrefors and Kosta Boda are owned by the same company, but the two firms still retain their individual identities. From 1950, with Vicke Lindstrand as artistic director, Kosta Boda enjoyed a particularly strong period with designers such as Mona Morales-Schildt, Erik Höglund, and later Signe Persson-Melin. While Orrefors prides itself on the purity of its glass, Kosta Boda has created a name for itself with richly colored glassware by designers like Ulrica Hydman-Vallien. Current designers at Kosta Boda include Gunnel Sahlin and Ann Wåhlström.

In the same region of southern Sweden as Orrefors and Kosta Boda (often referred to as "glasriket"—the glass country) sits a string of smaller glassworks such as Pukeberg, Lindshammar, Skruf, Nybro, Bergdala, and Åfors, some of them over a hundred years old. The Swedes are very proud of their glassmaking tradition, and visiting the glass country is a popular summer treat, offering an opportunity to see the glassblowers at work.

Finnish glass is very different from Swedish—less inviting and flirtatious, perhaps, but just as advanced and refined. Perhaps the best-known glass object in the world is the Savoy vase, designed by Alvar Aalto in 1936 and named after the Savoy restaurant in Helsinki and produced by the Finnish glassworks Iittala in the village of the same name. Iittala had a good designer in Göran Hongell, but with the arrival of Tapio Wirkkala and Kaj Franck in 1946, and Timo Sarpaneva in 1950, Iittala experienced a creative explosion. Sarpaneva

left First flowing, then frozen, the glassmaking process is reminiscent of the Scandinavian seascape. Here, decorative pieces from local glassworks are placed where they can catch the light.

right The magic of handmade glass is that each piece is always slightly different. Inspired by melting ice at the end of winter, this Finnish glass is close to nature in shape and color.

and Wirkkala created an endless series of both art glass and utility pieces for Iittala. Other talented designers such as Saara Hopea at Nuutajärvi, and Helena Tynell and Nanny Still at Riihimäki developed Finnish glass still further and made glass the most internationally celebrated Finnish design of the era.

Glass is still a source of national pride in Finland, but artistic glass production is no longer a priority at Iittala, which now owns Nuutajärvi. Instead, the focus is on mass-produced glassware for

this page The bark effect of this glass vase is typical of Timo Sarpaneva's work for Iittala during the 1960s. His later work is stricter in form.

right This pitcher by Kaj Franck from the Kartio series for Iittala was originally covered with rattan—highly decorative, but less practical once dishwashers were introduced.

opposite The Nappi (Button) tealight candle holders were designed by Markku Salo for Iittala in 1998. They are a good example of Iittala's current output of affordable, mass-made but nonetheless well-designed objects.

Glass is still a source of national pride in Finland, but art glass is no longer a priority at Iittala. Instead, the focus is on mass-produced domestic glassware.

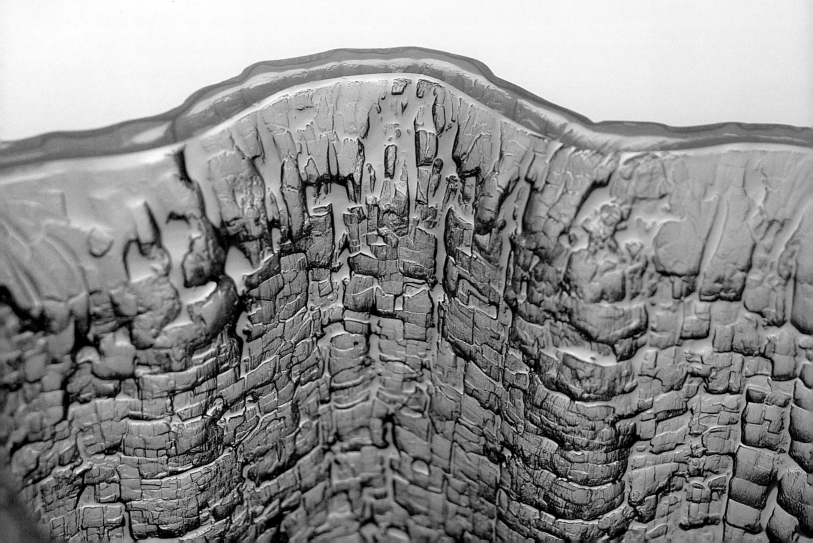

home use. Classics such as Kaj Franck's 1950s Kartio series and Aino Aalto's 1930s Aino series have been recently reissued by littala and are bestsellers once again, while contemporary designs by international names such as Konstantin Grcic and Alfredo Häberli continue littala's functionalist tradition. Some interesting glass is currently being produced at Riihimäki (home of the Finnish glass museum, created by Tapio Wirkkala) by independent designers such as Kristian Venäläinen and Pertti Metsälampi, but unfortunately it has limited distribution outside Finland.

Holmegaard and Kastrup enjoyed great success with contemporary glass during the 1950s and employed some of the best Danish designers of the time— Henning Koppel, Grethe Meyer, Nanna and Jørgen Ditzel, and Otto Brauer, to name but a few.

The main glassworks in Denmark are Holmegaard and its now-defunct sister factory Kastrup. In 1942, Holmegaard experienced a creative change with the arrival of a new artistic director, Per Lütken, whose numerous creations of the 1940s and 1950s are boldly organic and adventurously fluid in form. Both Holmegaard and Kastrup enjoyed great success with their contemporary glass during the 1950s and employed some of the best Danish designers of the time— Henning Koppel, Grethe Meyer, Nanna and Jørgen Ditzel, and Otto Brauer to name but a few. By the late 1960s, Holmegaard had gone distinctly pop, and even launched a line called Carnaby, but in 1979 the Kastrup factory closed down.

Today, Holmegaard is part of the Royal Scandinavia group, together with Orrefors Kosta Boda, but its direction seems uncertain. While vintage Holmegaard glass is highly collectible, the current glass production is mainly aimed at the home and tourist markets. This is also true of Hadeland, the most prominent Norwegian glassworks, where Arne Jon Jutrem was a strong name between 1950 and 1962.

opposite above Otto Brauer designed a series of large bottles while working at Holmegaard in the 1960s. Made in a multitude of colors, they are highly collectible today.

opposite below The Provence bowl, designed by Per Lütken in 1956 for Holmegaard, is still produced today. The bowl is made by pressing the hot mass of glass onto a wooden board soaked in water while quickly turning it, forcing the rapidly rising steam to create a cavity in the glass.

this page A glass vase and bowl by Per Lütken for Holmegaard share a table with a ceramic bowl by Stig Lindberg for Gustavsberg, Sweden. The free-form dish is typical of Lütken's organic shapes.

this page Curtains are often omitted when decorating Scandinavian houses, or are treated as a way of enhancing the light in a room rather than blocking it. Here, transparent linen panels are hung on a track so they can be moved easily.

opposite Two Poul Kjaerholm PK 22 chairs sit on a rug from IKEA designed by Eva Lilja Löwenhielm.

TEXTILES

The Scandinavians use textiles to bring warmth and interest to their interiors. Fabrics and rugs are a quick, colorful, and inexpensive way of transforming a room.

Although Nordic fashion houses like Denmark's In Wear and Sweden's Hennes & Mauritz are very successful, little clothing is manufactured in Scandinavia. However, many small but important textile manufacturers are dotted around the region, based around traditional, high-quality, and labor-intensive workshop production. Their great advantage is that they are able to create small series of fabrics and experiment with colors and designs.

The work of Austrian architect Josef Frank bridges the gap between traditional and modern Nordic style and between international and Scandinavian design. Married to a Swede in 1911, Frank immigrated from Germany to Sweden in 1934 to escape the Nazis. Even though Frank took modernism as his starting point, his work was very different from that of the Bauhaus-influenced designers. He favored natural materials such as cane and rattan, and curved forms instead of hard lines and right angles. As head designer for the company Svenskt Tenn and designer of the Swedish pavilion at the New York World Fair of 1939, Frank had a considerable influence. The upholstery and curtain textiles he created for Svenskt Tenn from the 1930s and 1940s are colorful and large-scale, but at the same time amazingly detailed, often revealing strong Asian influences. Botanic motifs were his great passion. Many of Frank's textile and furniture designs are still in production.

A master of form, line, and composition, Märta Måås-Fjetterström is another central figure in Swedish textile design. She started her own weaving workshop in 1919 and continued to run it until her death in 1941. A group of weavers has continued to realize Måås-Fjetterström's artistic intentions. For many years, Barbro Nilsson was the company's artistic leader, herself producing pieces that displayed supreme mastery of technique and revealed a deep feeling for color. Other artists have regularly contributed new designs that are produced by the talented in-house weavers. Today, fabrics and tapestries are still produced for clients across the world, and original Måås-Fjetterström work is highly priced at auction.

acclaimed work was produced in her own studio, including her herringbone- and goose-eye-patterned carpets and drapery of the 1950s as well as many other abstract handwoven pieces.

10-Gruppen (10 Swedish Designers) was formed in 1970 as a response to a creative and commercial crisis in the Swedish textile industry that stemmed from a lack of innovation and increased international competition. Most of the designers involved were already established names, but all shared the belief that the large textile companies did not appreciate the need for good modern design. 10-Gruppen's members included Inez Svensson, Ingela Håkansson, Gunilla Axén, Tom Hedqvist, and Birgitta Hahn. 10-Gruppen's prints are bold and colorful. Although 10-Gruppen is not a large company, it has made a big impact, producing designs that have sold through IKEA, Habitat, Paul Smith, and the Swedish Coop. Thanks to a 30th-anniversary exhibition at the Swedish National Museum, 10-Gruppen has recently come back into focus.

Possibly the most celebrated Scandinavian textile company is Marimekko, founded in Finland in 1951 by Armi and Viljo Ratia.

Since its opening in 1902, Nordiska Kompaniet (NK) has been the leading department store in Stockholm. Between 1937 and 1971, NK had its own textile-manufacturing division. Astrid Sampe was head of the design studio, where she created a wealth of innovative printed and woven fabrics. She also employed numerous other talented designers, including Stig Lindberg, Sven Markelius, Viola Gråsten, Olle Baertling, and Arne Jacobsen. Sampe also created rugs for the United Nations building in New York and was friendly with American designers such as Charles Eames, Eero Saarinen, and Florence Knoll.

A contemporary of Sampe, Ingrid Dessau, designed rugs for the carpet manufacturer Kasthall between 1954 and 1978 and fabrics for Kinnasand between 1970 and 1984. However, some of her most

above left Pia Wallén has returned to a simple cross shape in several of her designs, like this hand-tufted wool rug for Asplund. It can be interpreted as a symbol of positivity: a large plus sign.

right Wood fibers mixed with cotton make a strong material, as in these Ritva Puotila cushions for Woodnotes. The fibers are so dense that little dust can settle into the fabric.

opposite This wood fiber rug by Ritva Puotila is a natural companion to wooden furniture and shows that there are still ways of developing new products based on traditional Scandinavian manufacturing methods.

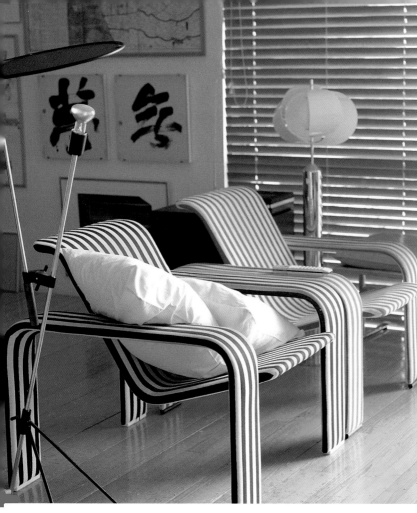

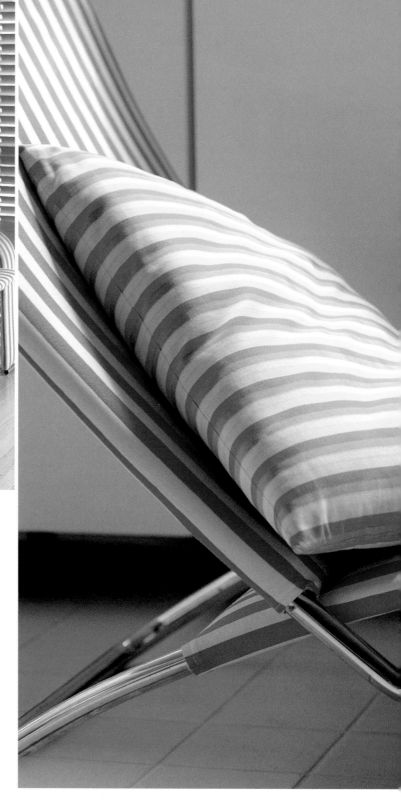

Along with Nanna Ditzel, whose Hallingdal fabric for the company Kvadrat is a modern Danish classic, Vibeke Klint is the best-known Danish textile designer of the last 50 years. Klint designed rugs and mass-produced curtain and upholstery fabric. Her colorful abstract designs drew inspiration from India and the Klint textile tradition of traditional materials and techniques and simple patterns, which has dominated Danish textile design. Her student Kim Naver developed Vibeke Klint's style still further with her work for Georg Jensen Damask, a Danish textile company (and no relation to the silvermaker).

Possibly the most celebrated Scandinavian textile company is Marimekko, founded in Finland in 1951 by Armi and Viljo Ratia. Marimekko's real breakthrough came with the 1960 US presidential election campaign between Kennedy and Nixon. Conservative

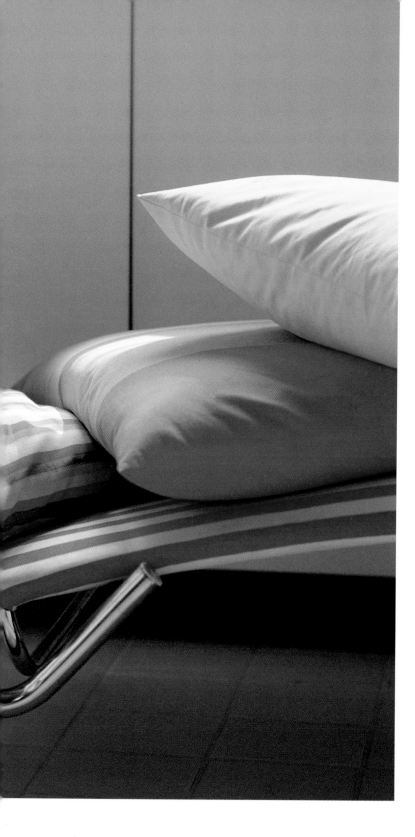

opposite and left These chairs for fashion company Vuokko by Antti Nurmesniemi are upholstered in a fabric by Vuokko Nurmesniemi. The striped Piccolo fabric she designed for Marimekko in 1953 was followed by Annika Rimala's Tasaraita stripe in 1968. The French might be regarded as the inventors of striped tops, but thanks to Marimekko, the Finns have an even closer relation to stripes— bedlinen, fabric, clothes, dishes, and bags have all been produced in jaunty and colorful stripes. In 2001, the Finnish postal service released a Marimekko striped stamp. Jackie Kennedy wore cotton dresses by Vuokko Nurmesniemi in the early 1960s, and Annika Rimala personally sold her a striped shirt later in the decade. At one point Levi's offered to produce Annika Rimala's striped designs, but she politely declined.

right Maija Isola designed some of Marimekko's all-time classics, including the Kaivo fabric (above) and Unikko flower (below). Her large-scale designs in bold colors forced Marimekko to develop new printing techniques to match the large areas of color. Several Maija Isola designs are in the permanent collection of the Museum of Modern Art (MoMA) in New York.

newspapers had criticized Jacqueline Kennedy for her penchant for expensive French designer clothing, so when she bought some colorful Finnish cotton dresses from a shop in Cape Cod, the story was printed in some 200 newspapers all over the country. As a result, Marimekko became an instant success story.

Something between a company and a cult, Marimekko's mission was to produce colorful and comfortable clothing at affordable prices. It employed some of the most talented Finnish textile designers of its time, including Vuokko Nurmesniemi, Annika Rimala, and Maija Isola. After a period of decline during the 1980s, Marimekko is now right back in fashion and reprinting many of its archive designs, such as Maija Isola's Unikko flower print from 1965, which has become something of a Marimekko trademark.

left Danish ceramics are produced
and developed in small studios as well
as by larger companies. These vases
from 1997 were made by Bodil Manz
in her own studio.

above Stackability is a theme that
several Scandinavian designers have
returned to again and again, in glass,
plastic, and ceramics. These bowls are
from Grethe Meyer's Blå Kant series .

CERAMICS

The innovative glazes, colors, and designs of modern Scandinavian ceramics means that they have few international competitors.

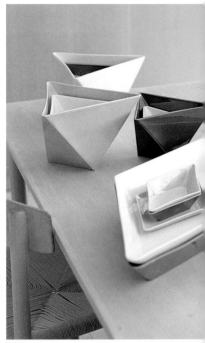

Some major changes have taken place in the Scandinavian ceramics industry over the last 50 years, with several mergers and closures of many once-prominent manufacturers. Nowadays, notable ceramics are often produced by independent designers working from small studios and are sold through galleries.

Nevertheless, Danish ceramics are largely synonymous with two companies, Den Kongelige Porcelainsfabrik (the Royal Porcelain Factory), founded in 1775, and Bing & Grøndahl, founded in 1853. In 1987 these two august old firms were merged under the name Royal Copenhagen. During the first golden age of Danish ceramics in the 1880s, both companies developed an Asian-inspired but distinctively Danish style. With the arrival of the functionalist style in the 1930s, Danish ceramics enjoyed a second golden era that continued until well after World War II, when Danish Modern became a byword for Scandinavian design. The designer Axel Salto was a key figure in Danish ceramics from the 1930s to the 1950s, along with other acclaimed designers such as Henning Koppel, Gertrud Vasegaard, and Grethe Meyer.

Den Kongelige Porcelainsfabrik and Bing & Grøndahl never dominated Danish ceramics in the way that large manufacturers dominated the ceramic industries in Sweden and Finland. In Denmark there were also numerous small independent potteries. Saxbo existed from 1930 until 1968 with the talented studio potters Nathalie Krebs and Eva Staehr-Nielsen in charge. The famous Kähler family produced pottery for four generations, from 1839 until 1969. Other notable firms included Palshus, Søholm, Holbaek, Humlebaek, and Nymølle. Many of the smaller potteries developed a simple, rustic, handcrafted style that is much sought today.

above right **These rectangular dishes by Grethe Meyer are named Side By Side and were designed for Royal Copenhagen in 1996, but never put into production.**

below right **A group of experimental pottery vessels by Finn Juhl stands on a windowsill in the home he shared with Hanne Wilhelm Hansen (see pages 82–87)**

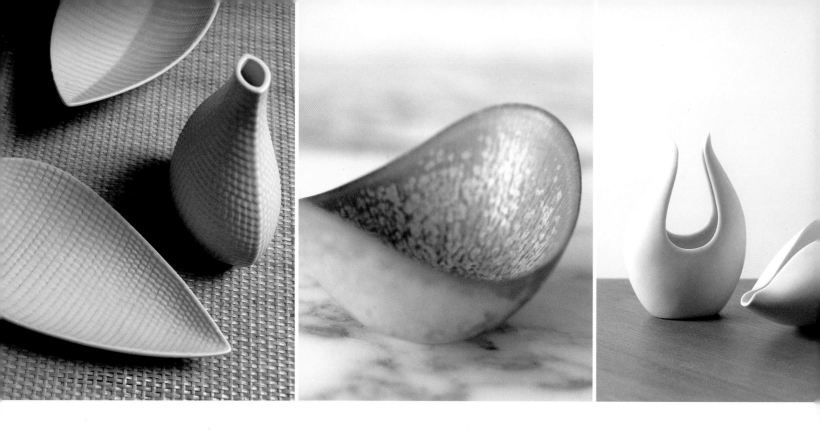

The 1930s to the 1960s was a golden period for Rörstrand and its two talented main designers, Gunnar Nylund and Carl-Harry Stålhane.

The 1970s and 1980s were not a good period for Danish ceramics, due to growing international competition and fading interest in the Danish Modern style. Royal Copenhagen's response was to reissue a series of classic pieces dating from the 19th century. However, Ole Jensen has recently produced some good work for Royal Copenhagen, which suggests there may be a brighter future for the company. Nowadays, the best way to find interesting Danish ceramics is to visit the small studios and workshops dotted across Denmark.

Founded in Stockholm in 1726, Rörstrand is Europe's second oldest ceramic factory. The 1930s to the 1960s was a golden period for Rörstrand and its two main designers, Gunnar Nylund and Carl-Harry Stålhane, who worked on both studio and production wares. With the decline in popularity of the Scandinavian Modern style in the 1970s, the design department was closed down, and in 1983, Rörstrand was bought by the Finnish company Designor.

During the 20th century, Gustavsberg, the other leading Swedish ceramics manufacturer, employed perhaps the most interesting ceramic designers of the time, including Willhelm Kåge, Stig Lindberg,

above, from left to right Dishes and
a vase by Stig Lindberg for Gustavsberg;
a bowl by Gunnar Nylund for Rörstrand;
white vessels by Stig Lindberg and
Gunnar Nylund. Lindberg was also
active as an illustrator and produced
several popular children's books. The
work of both designers has become
increasingly sought in recent years,
not least in the United States, where
mid-20th-century Swedish ceramics
are highly appreciated.

right The Cirrus stoneware vase is
designed by Pia Törnell and made at
Rörstrand. It requires a mold with
13 different parts. Pia Törnell is perhaps
the most interesting designer currently
working for Rörstrand.

opposite below The Suomi (Finland)
series was designed by Timo Sarpaneva
in 1974 for the German company
Rosenthal. It quickly became one of
the company's bestsellers and has
been developed further with various
colors and patterns. The pure white
version is the one that does the
Bauhaus-inspired design most justice.

and Bernt Friberg. Founded in 1827, Gustavsberg is situated outside Stockholm on the Baltic Sea, where it received shipments of clay from England to manufacture its bone china. Owned by the Swedish Co-op from the 1930s, Gustavsberg began to produce porcelain-enameled steel for ovens, refrigerators, and sanitaryware. It also produced enameled porcelain studio pieces. In the 1980s the factory was bought by Designor and closed down soon after.

Today, a small group of independent potters continue production at Gustavsberg, including the designer Ingegerd Råman. She also designs for Figgjo, a Norwegian company that has become the largest ceramic manufacturer in Scandinavia, supplying schools, hospitals, and restaurants. Despite their focus on utility china, Figgjo produced many interesting designs during the 1950s and 1960s, and still maintains a high standard of design. The other leading Norwegian ceramics

left The long, shallow decorated dish is typical of the playful designs Stig Lindberg produced for Gustavsberg.

below The Teema series by Kaj Franck was originally introduced under the name Kilta in 1953. The bottle with a cork stopper is a milk jug. Its base was designed to fit snugly between the inner and outer panes of a standard double-glazed Finnish window (in the 1950s both refrigerators and triple glazing were still unusual in Finland). In 1975, Arabia's new owners changed the factory's production from earthenware (which is not oven- or microwave-proof) to stoneware, and the earthenware Kilta series was discontinued, despite the fact that 25 million pieces had been sold. The protests that followed in Finland made national news, and in 1981 the series was reintroduced in stoneware under the name Teema.

right These Gustavsberg pieces combine functional design with bold patterns.

With a 374-foot kiln—for a while the largest in the world—and over a thousand employees, the Finnish company Arabia was the biggest ceramic manufacturer in Europe during the late 1930s.

factory, Porsgrund, enjoyed great success with Nora Gulbrandsen as artistic director before the war and with Tias Eckhoff during the 1950s. Nowadays, the focus is on the mainstream domestic market.

Finnish ceramics is dominated by Arabia, which was founded in 1873 as a subsidiary to Rörstrand, but which has been under Finnish ownership since 1916. With a 374-foot kiln—for a while the largest in the world—and over a thousand employees, Arabia was the biggest

ceramic manufacturer in Europe during the late 1930s. Despite its being a large-scale commercial manufacturer, the artistic director Kurt Ekholm set up an art department where 30 artists had freedom to experiment without commercial constraints. In 1946, Kaj Franck took over as artistic director and surrounded himself with a number of other talents, such as Ulla Procopé, Birger Kaipiainen, Oiva Toikka, and Ulla Bryk (wife of Tapio Wirkkala). Franck's Kilta series from 1953 (reissued as Teema in 1981) may well be the most famous Arabia product, its spare, simple lines encapsulating the essence of Scandinavian functionalism. Recent Arabia products include Ego by Stefan Lindfors and ABC by Pekka Harni.

METAL

In Scandinavia, metal has been transformed into decorative objects since the time of the Vikings. Indeed, Viking silver, with its simple shapes and bold patterns, has had a huge influence on modern Scandinavian metalware.

The Danish firm Georg Jensen is one of the world's most famous silver manufacturers. Jensen himself retired in 1926, by which time the company employed hundreds of silversmiths (compared to some two dozen today). Early Jensen silver is of superb quality. The company enjoyed a second peak of popularity from the 1950s on, producing work by celebrated designers such as Henning Koppel, Jørgen and Nanna Ditzel, Bent Gabrielsen, and Magnus Stephensen, all of whom also worked in steel. Henning Koppel's fish dish in silver has become something of an icon for modern Danish silversmiths. Georg Jensen's main competitor, A. Michelsen, employed the architects Kay Fisker and Ib Lunding, and originally produced Arne Jacobsen's steel flatware for the SAS Royal Hotel before Georg Jensen bought the company.

Unsurprising given their skill with silver, the Danes are equally talented when it comes to stainless steel. Arne Jacobsen's Cylinda Line for Stelton dates from 1967. The pieces are made from large sheets of steel that are bent into cylindrical shapes and hand polished. The end result is a series of sleek, minimalist objects reminiscent of Bauhaus silverware. Stelton followed up the Cylinda Line with designs by Erik Magnussen, who created a simple but brilliant vacuum jug that is a standard feature in most Danish offices.

At the beginning of the 20th century, Swedish silver was less decorative than that made in the Danish style, with some austerely beautiful jewelry, church decorations, and flatware being produced by Jacob Ängman and later Erik Fleming, Wiwen Nilsson, and Sigvard Bernadotte. Sigurd Persson worked silver, gold, and stones into

opposite **This Arne Jacobsen teapot was produced by Stelton in 1967, part of Jacobsen's Cylinda Line. Creating this line required a monumental product development exercise on the part of Stelton's owner, Peter Holmblad (Arne Jacobsen's stepson). Details such as the non-drip lip and the seamless join between the spout and main body reveal the high level of finish and the perfection of each piece.**

above **Stelton developed several products with Erik Magnussen, such as this minimalist flatware.**

right **Silver company Georg Jensen also produces stainless steel flatware, like these spoons by Grethe Meyer.**

modern styles and developed his shapes through his industrial designs for flatware, pots, glasses, and even such humble objects such as kitchen brushes. The popular jewelry designs of Vivianna Torun Bülow-Hübe are mainly associated with Georg Jensen, which still produces her classic steel bangle wristwatch from 1969, but the Swedish jewelry designer had her own studio in Stockholm in the 1950s before moving to France and later Asia.

Over the past few years, the stainless-steel kitchenware produced by Finnish firm Hackman has received much favorable attention. Designs by international names such as Renzo Piano and Antonio Citterio have set a new standard for flatware, pans, and kitchen utensils. The most celebrated Finnish silversmith of the past century is Bertel Gardberg, a master in silver, gold, brass, and stainless steel as well as wood and glass. Gardberg's work can be found in many Finnish homes in the shape of the Carelia flatware he designed for

Hackman. His student, Börje Rajalin, has been chief designer at the silver company Kalevala Koru since 1956, but he is also an industrial designer responsible for trains, ferries, and even the Helsinki metro.

In the early 1960s, the Finnish sculptor and jewelry designer Björn Weckström's discovery of some gold nuggets in Lapland sparked a whole new style of jewelry design. A forerunner in his field, Weckström broke with the traditional concepts of jewelry design by boldly combining different materials. Since 1963, Weckström has worked for the silver company Lapponia. Poul Havgaard, a Danish blacksmith and jewelry designer, began a long association with Lapponia in 1971. Havgaard made his name in the 1960s, when he produced unique pieces of jewelry and sculptures forged from iron and steel. He still creates these pieces in his workshop on the island of Fyn in Denmark.

During the 1950s and 1960s, Norwegian silver designers were among the most progressive in Scandinavia, particularly those linked to the company David-Andersen AS. Harry Sørby joined the company in 1929 and designed for them right up to the 1970s, developing his style from classicism through functionalism into Scandinavian Modern. Norwegian silversmiths were particularly innovative in their use of enamel, which was used to create almost psychedelic patterns by designers like Torbjørn Lie-Jørgensen and Uni David-Andersen. Another popular Norwegian innovation was cast silver, used by Unn Tangerud to make geometric-shaped pendants, often set with Norwegian stones such as thulite. Norwegian flatware was also a great export during the 1950s, not least the Maya flatware series designed by Tias Eckhoff for Norsk Stålpress.

During the 1950s and 1960s, Norwegian silver designers were among the most progressive in Scandinavia, particularly those linked to the company David-Andersen AS.

opposite Metal outdoor furniture designed by Antti Nurmesniemi stands on the terrace of Antti and Vuokko Nurmesniemi's home.

above This lamp, model 1005, is Erik Magnussen's latest addition to a long line of designs he has produced for the Danish company Stelton. Many of Magnussen's metal designs are developments or refinements of ideas he originally had when working with ceramics for Bing & Grøndahl. Magnussen has also worked in silver for Georg Jensen and Selangor.

right The ship's lamp, model 1001 by Erik Magnussen, continues the minimal cylindrical theme for Stelton. The metal ring positioned around the glass can be manually adjusted to block out the glare of the naked flame and it has the added advantages of both heating and dehumidifying onboard.

this page The Formula chair is the latest in a long series of witty designs in plastic by the Finnish designer Eero Aarnio. Because it is plastic, the chair can also be used outdoors. Note the space to hold drink cans in the side.

PLASTIC

The Italians enjoyed tremendous success with plastics during the 1960s and 1970s. Two Scandinavians also developed a reputation for their groundbreaking designs in plastic: Eero Aarnio and Verner Panton.

Many Nordic industrial designers also worked in plastic, not least Sigvard Bernadotte, a Swedish royal prince and multitalented designer who also worked in silver, ceramics, glass, graphics, and textiles. Bernadotte was one of the founders of the Swedish Industrial Designers Society and was also for many years president of ICSID, the International Council of Societies of Industrial Design. His plastic nesting Margrethe mixing bowls, designed for the Danish company Rosti in 1950, are still in production more than half a century later. (In fact, the bowls were dreamed up by Bernadotte's young assistant Jacob Jensen, who was later to make Bang & Olufsen famous with his sleek hi-fi designs.)

Another Bernadotte success story was the plastic Röda Klara wall-mounted can opener, which has been a standard piece of equipment in every Swedish kitchen for a quarter of a century.

right The Margrethe mixing bowl by the Danish company Rosti was created by Jacob Jensen in 1950 while he was working for the designers Sigvard Bernadotte and Acton Bjørn. It has been in production ever since. To celebrate its 50th anniversary, Rosti commissioned a bowl in silver as a gift for Queen Margrethe of Denmark.

far right The Vitra Design Museum has produced a miniature of Eero Aarnio's Ball chair, which the designer proudly displays in his home. Sitting inside the large chair blocks out all surrounding sounds.

Bernadotte's influence on Swedish design has been profound—even the exact shade of blue on the cars on the Stockholm Metro was only chosen after consultation with Bernadotte.

The Finnish designer Eero Aarnio opened his interior- and industrial-design studio in Helsinki in 1962. In 1963, he designed the futuristic Ball chair (also known as the Thunderball or Globe): a round sphere made from molded polyester-reinforced fiberglass. Its material and form made it a complete novelty for the furniture industry of the time, even though fiberglass was already used in boat construction. The easy-to-work material enabled Aarnio to create

left The Panthella floor lamp is produced by Louis Poulsen. It was originally introduced in a variety of different colors, but the current production is only in white, lending it a timeless, classic air.

right Nanna Ditzel created several pieces for the Danish company Domus Danica in the late 1960s, including this chair, which was produced in several different colors and versions.

furniture in unusual forms without restrictions. With his Pastil, Bubble and Tomato chairs, Aarnio received international acclaim as furniture designer to the pop generation. The chairs can be used both indoors and out, and they float on water. They have been featured in numerous films over the last thirty years. Aarnio is still active as a designer, and his most famous work is now in production again.

The well-known futuristic designs in plastic of Danish designer Verner Panton range from the stacking molded-plastic Panton chair—the first example of a single-form molded fiberglass chair (now made in polyurethane)—to the acrylic Panthella lamps he created for Louis Poulsen, to inflatable furniture and even attempts to create plastic houses. Although Panton will always be associated with his innovative space-age designs of the 1960s, in reality his career spanned five productive decades. As trends in interiors shift away from minimal white interiors, the color, energy, and *joie de vivre* of Panton's designs have won them a new popularity.

The well-known futuristic designs in plastic of Danish designer Verner Panton range from the stacking molded-plastic Panton chair—the first example of a single-form molded chair—to his acrylic Panthella lamps.

right The Panton chair of 1960 signaled the beginning of the era of plastic furniture, but the concept of a chair crafted from a single piece of material had occupied several Danish designers throughout the 1950s.

LIGHT

The Nordic summer nights are warm and light, while the winter months are long and dark with only a few hours of weak sun every day. As a result, maximizing quality of light has been a preoccupation of many Scandinavian architects and designers.

opposite and below left
Poul Henningsen's model PH 5 from 1958 is just one in a long series of PH lamps, which started back in 1926. It has become the most popular model and is said to hang in half of all Danish homes.

right Because Scandinavia lies in the north of the northern hemisphere, and the sun hits the ground at an angle rather than from above, the light is diffused and weakened. As a result, maximizing light is always a priority in Scandinavian architecture. This room has two glass walls and enjoys the luxury of natural daylight throughout the day.

The Danish architect, designer, and writer Poul Henningsen is unique in terms of the sheer volume of his lighting designs. Born in 1894, he designed his first PH light in the 1920s in cooperation with the company Louis Poulsen, and continued to work right up until his death in 1967. Henningsen was a political radical, and his co-operation with Louis Poulsen was only possible due to the equally radical outlook of its managing director Sosphus Kaastrup-Olsen. Both men saw it as their mission to bring electrical power and good quality lighting to the masses—most working-class homes at the time had no electrical supply at all, or only a naked light bulb.

By the 1930s, the PH lamps were bestsellers, and many models are still in production today. The principle is simple—a carefully constructed shade screens the glare of the bulb while distributing light evenly around the room. The PH lamps appear in many Danish homes and public buildings, as well as in the work of Danish architects around the world, including the Sydney Opera House.

left and far left **Le Klint's** hand-folded paper lampshades were given a bold new look by Poul Christensen in the 1970s.

this page **The PH Plate** pendant, designed by Poul Henningsen, was produced by Louis Poulsen up until the mid-1980s.

Most designs are discreet and classical, but Le Klint's collaboration with designer Poul Christiansen in the 1970s resulted in some playful, pop-art styles.

The only other lamps that have managed to compete with PH lamps in Danish homes are those produced by Le Klint, a small but successful family company. Founded in 1943 by Tage Klint, brother of the famous Danish furniture designer Kaare Klint, the company has worked with dozens of designers over the years to produce shades fashioned from hand-folded plastic. Most designs are discreet and classical in feel, but Le Klint's collaboration with designer Poul Christiansen in the 1970s resulted in some playful, pop-art styles that have recently enjoyed a new lease on life.

Arne Jacobsen was a close friend of Poul Henningsen's (they escaped the German occupation of Denmark together by crossing to Sweden in a row boat with their wives), and he was undoubtedly influenced by Henningsen's research into lighting distribution, especially as most of Jacobsen's lights were also produced by Louis Poulsen. Although Jacobsen is better known as a furniture designer and architect nowadays, he produced a large number of lighting designs that were used for several specific architectural projects.

this page The Stelling mouth-blown glass pendant is an early Arne Jacobsen design, manufactured by Louis Poulsen for the Stelling house in Copenhagen in 1937. The lamp was briefly reproduced during 2002 as part of the Arne Jacobsen centenary celebration and is already a collector's item.

this page and opposite left The AJ table and floor lamps were designed by Arne Jacobsen and made by Louis Poulsen for the SAS Royal Hotel, Copenhagen. The circular foot was designed to hold an ashtray. The thin stem was a difficult achievement at a time when electrical wiring was thicker than it is today.

right **Arne Jacobsen** designed St. Catherine's College in Oxford, England, in the early 1960s. The Oxford lamp was designed for the students' reading desks and was mounted directly into the wooden tables without a foot. Louis Poulsen later made a limited production of the lamp with a circular foot.

The Stelling glass pendant of 1937 was briefly reissued in 2002, but otherwise only a few of his lights are still in production, such as the AJ lamp series created for the SAS Royal Hotel in Copenhagen and the Munkegard ceiling lamp for the Munkegard school. Some Jacobsen lamps have been reissued by Spanish company Santa & Cole, including the Aarhus lamp, designed for Aarhus city hall in the 1930s.

Finnish designers have expended great effort on their lighting designs. Alvar Aalto was another friend of Henningsen's and adapted the idea of a multishade system to suit his own architectural style. Like Jacobsen, he created most of his lighting designs for specific architectural projects, and many are still in production by his company Artek, which he founded in the 1930s. Tapio Wirkkala also worked on lighting designs, as did the Le Corbusier-trained designer Ilmari Tapiovaara, but the most prolific Finnish lighting designer was Lisa Johansson-Pape. Born in 1907, she originally trained and worked as a furniture designer. In 1930 she visited the Stockholm exhibition,

Although Arne Jacobsen is better known as a furniture designer and architect, he designed a large number of lights for specific projects.

opposite far left **The PH Snowball was designed by Poul Henningsen for Louis Poulsen in 1958.**

far left **When Verner Panton first designed the Panthella lamps for Louis Poulsen, he used the same size shade for the table and floor lamps, but soon realized that the proportions did not work. Later table lamps, like this one, have smaller shades.**

left **The Moon lamp was designed by Verner Panton for Louis Poulsen in the 1960s. The overlapping shade is reminiscent of Poul Henningsen's designs for the Copenhagen Tivoli for blackouts during the war, so that no light was visible from the air.**

which was a turning point in her life. From the 1940s she worked for the Orno lighting factory and designed an endless series of glass, textile, metal, and plastic lamps, both for home and public use. Johansson-Pape was skilled at tastefully and tactfully installing contemporary lighting in historical buildings, a talent which won her the job of lighting consultant to the great mosque in Mecca during the 1970s. Her expertise in lighting took her on lecture tours and exhibitions around the world, and there are many Finnish homes that still use Johansson-Pape lights manufactured by Orno.

Another great Orno lighting designer was Yki Nummi, the son of a Finnish missionary born in China in 1925. Between 1950 and 1958, for Orno, he designed lamps for hospitals, sanatoriums, churches, and offices. Between 1951 and 1965, Nummi developed a series of transparent acrylic lamps; the Modern Art table lamp from 1956 was exhibited at MoMA, while his futuristic Sky Flyer from 1960 is now back in production again.

Luxo is the largest lighting company in Norway, built on the success of its founder, Jac Jacobsen (no relation to Arne Jacobsen), and his L-1 desk lamp, designed in 1937. The L-1 was principally an adaptation of earlier Bauhaus designs, but Jacobsen managed to improve both the function and esthetics of the light. The concept of two jointed arms controlled by springs and with a heavy base or clamp to hold the lamp in place has now become a standard design for almost all desk lamps. For a while during the 1940s and 1950s, the Luxo L-1 dominated the world market in desk lamps, and its success has helped Luxo to become a world leader in lighting designed especially for the workplace.

For a while during the 1940s and 1950s, the L-1 dominated the world market in desk lamps, and its success has helped Luxo to become a world leader in lighting designed especially for the workplace.

above Danish designer Finn Juhl experimented with product design outside furniture, but only a handful of pieces made it into production. This table lamp from 1963 was produced by the Danish company Lyfa. The bottom part of the shade can be tilted to adjust the direction of the light.

opposite The Norwegian company Luxo made many different versions of the L–1 desk lamp, designed by the company's founder Jac Jacobsen. The basic principle of two arms and a spring system was a German invention, but Jacobsen added some Scandinavian design talent and successful marketing.

living

this page The south-facing window is a single 160-square-foot sheet of glass that allows natural light to flood in extravagantly. The sea is only about 75 yards away, lying just the other side of the fringe of wild grass that has been planted around the house. The sofa and desk are from Cappellini; the floor lamp is an Arne Jacobsen design for Louis Poulsen.

Mikael Andersen

Built like a strictly symmetrical wooden box, this unique building is situated close to the sea on Nordsjælland in Denmark.

When gallery owner Mikael Andersen wanted to create a haven of tranquility where his artist friends could work without distraction, he called on one of the world's most celebrated architects, the legendary Henning Larsen. It is unusual for such a well-known and long-established architect to undertake a small-scale house project, but it is obvious that this project was something of a labor of love for Larsen. His building stands in a grove of larch trees and is surrounded by 200 newly planted birches.

Henning Larsen worked for two of the greatest names in Danish 20th-century architecture—Arne Jacobsen and Jørn Utzon—before he set up his own studio in 1959. Today he employs over 100 people. His most famous building is the Saudi Arabian Foreign Ministry in Riyadh, a monumental, fortresslike structure that marries together Danish and Islamic styles. Recent projects include the Danish Design Center and the new Opera House in Copenhagen.

The house he designed for Andersen is a single space of 1,000 square feet. A freestanding kitchen and toilet area in the center divides the space into two halves: an artists' studio and a living area. If necessary, sliding doors can divide the interior into four rooms. Large terraces run along two sides of the house. Larsen is known for his unique way of working with light by bringing daylight into buildings. His work

this page At the center of the space is a small self-contained kitchen and toilet area with a fireplace on each side. The walls and ceiling are covered with laminated birch.

opposite above left Along the side of the building, five sections of the wall can be opened and closed individually to control the flow of light.

opposite center left Four sliding doors can divide the house into four sections. The aluminum chairs are for use both on the terrace outside and inside the house.

opposite below left The kitchen is small but well planned. The stainless-steel handles on the cupboards were designed by Arne Jacobsen in the late 1960s for the National Bank in Copenhagen.

opposite above right The concept of the house is to function as a retreat for Danish and international artists. With its quiet surroundings and excellent natural lighting, the house allows the guests to focus entirely on their work.

Mikael Andersen wanted to create a haven of tranquility where his artist friends could work without distraction.

around the world means that he has been able to study the way light falls in different countries. In the northern hemisphere, the sun comes in at an angle and creates a soft, translucent light, so people strive to let in as much daylight as possible. In the house Larsen has created for Mikael Andersen, this aim is particularly evident. The largest window in the house faces south and is 160 square feet in size. On the long side of the building, five sections of the wood-sided wall can be raised to let the daylight flood in. When closed, the building resembles a boat with all the hatches tightly battened down for a storm.

below left The house is clad in larch wood and has a flat roof that is angled just enough to drain off rainwater.

left Along the outside of the house, five hatches can be opened to allow in varying amounts of natural daylight.

this page Andersen's neighbors have affectionately named the house the cigar box. The surrounding land has been planted with 200 birch trees and plenty of wild grass.

left As in many Danish houses, the stove is a freestanding feature.

right On top of the bookshelves stand glass prototypes by Grethe Meyer. The sofa, model 2213, was designed by Børge Mogensen in 1962 for his own home, and is now produced by Fredericia Furniture. It is Mogensen's bestselling sofa and is a standard in Danish embassies around the world. The coffee table is another Mogensen classic, also dating from 1962. In front is Mogensen's easy chair model 2254 from 1958, covered with fabric designed by Lis Ahlmann.

Grethe Meyer

Grethe Meyer's home showcases objects she created as Denmark's foremost ceramic designer as well as furniture designed by her friend Børge Mogensen.

Grethe Meyer's home was designed in the 1960s by a group of Danish architects. It is characteristic of its time, with simple white brickwork and an open floor plan. Whitewashed floorboards provide a restrained backdrop for the furniture. Many pieces are by celebrated Danish designer Børge Mogensen (see pages 94–99). Meyer and Mogensen were close friends and collaborated on several furniture projects.

The two designers shared many beliefs and ideals. Like Mogensen's, Grethe Meyer's work espouses practicality, simplicity, and harmony. Their joint work for the Danish Consumer Cooperative during the 1950s attempted to provide people with

left and right The large shelving unit is filled with a beautiful collection of old and new ceramics, all designed by Grethe Meyer. The large, rounded bowls are part of her Blå Kant (Blue Line) collection. Suspended above the table is the PH 5 hanging lamp by Poul Henningsen; one is said to hang in one out of two Danish homes. The Shaker table and chairs are by Børge Mogensen for the Danish Consumer Cooperative in 1944.

Meyer's home is practical, unpretentious, and comfortable. The countless pieces of china and glass—all her own designs—are not precious objects to be handled with care. Instead, they are used just as Meyer intended them to be—every single day.

inexpensive yet good-quality furniture that could be sold as standardized modules. The best-known result of their efforts is the Boligens Byggeskape wall unit, which dates from 1952 and is now a modern classic.

Grethe Meyer trained as an architect, but since the 1960s her best-known work has been in ceramics, mainly for Royal Copenhagen. At a time when the highly decorative style of the 1950s began to fall from favor, Meyer's simple, rustic designs were in tune with public taste. Today her functionalist style is popular once more. Her faience tableware series Blå Kant (Blue Line) of 1965 provided Royal Copenhagen with

above left The Øresund kitchen system, designed by Børge Mogensen and Grethe Meyer, displays a collection of Meyer's own ceramics. When the Blå Kant (Blue Line) series was introduced in 1965, the line came in a single color, but today the series has been renamed 4 All Seasons and comes in a multitude of different shades, as can be seen on the two top shelves.

above right The brass hanging lamp is another of Meyer's own designs. It hangs in front of stacks of teacups from the Blå Kant series.

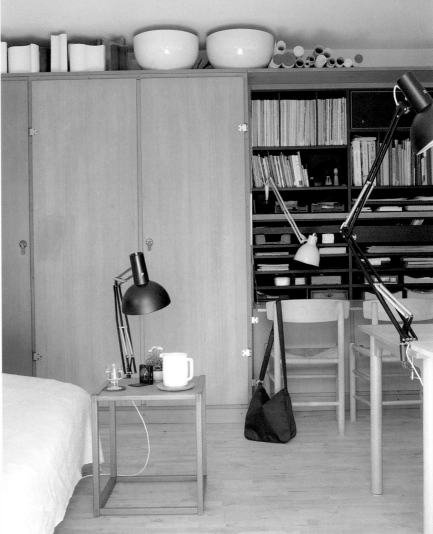

left The 1952 Boligens Byggeskape wall unit was designed by Grethe Meyer and Børge Mogensen. It became a bestseller and broke new ground in modular storage systems. The rectangular Side by Side dishes were made by Grethe Meyer for Royal Copenhagen in 1996 but never put into mass production.

above Blå Kant (Blue Line) bowls and Ocean vases by Grethe Meyer are ranged along the top shelf. The side table is by Børge Mogensen.

a bestseller that is still sold to this day (under the name 4 All Seasons). The same is true of her Hvidpot (White Pot) series of 1971. Another popular Meyer design is the stainless-steel Copenhagen flatware designed for Georg Jensen in 1991.

Grethe Meyer's home reflects her design ethos. It is practical, unpretentious, and very comfortable. The countless pieces of china and glass—all her own designs—are not treated as precious objects to be handled with care. Instead, they are used just as Meyer intended them to be—every single day.

this page The large
Kuutti Lavonen painting
is entitled Regina Celi.
Stacked on the floor are
two large cushions from
the Woodnotes collection.
Outside, the balcony runs
the whole length of the
living room.

right The dining table is by
Antonio Citterio for B&B
Italia, while the wood-fiber
rugs from the Woodnotes
collection were designed
by Ritva Puotila.

Mikko Puotila

With a new floor plan, an ordinary apartment in Espoo, Finland, has been transformed into an open-plan space that offers flexible and comfortable family living.

Mikko Puotila runs Woodnotes, a company he set up with his mother, the Finnish textile designer Ritva Puotila. Her large-scale textile artworks can be seen in many institutions and corporate headquarters both in Finland and abroad. Ritva Puotila first begun experimenting with wood fiber as a textile material in the 1960s, and in the late 1980s she and Mikko Puotila took the bold decision to establish a company producing items made from the material.

When Ritva and Mikko Puotila set up their company, wood fiber was a deeply unfashionable, utilitarian material, associated with hard times. Wood fiber had been used in Finland to replace imported cotton in wartime and was also used to insulate underground telephone cables. The Puotilas managed to purchase the last factory in Finland specializing in wood-fiber insulated cables, and converted the

this page With simple china and a Woodnotes runner, the table setting has an oriental flavor. The tall console table offers display space, but also keeps treasures out of the reach of tiny fingers. The cube bookshelves were custom made.

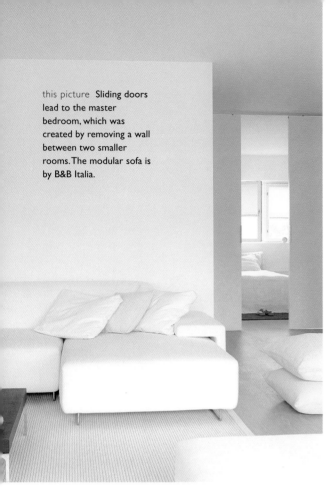

this picture **Sliding doors lead to the master bedroom, which was created by removing a wall between two smaller rooms. The modular sofa is by B&B Italia.**

this picture **The kitchen has a sea view, but the main work surface overlooks the living room. Black Series 7 chairs and an Eero Saarinen Tulip table with an Italian Arabescato marble top are used for informal meals.**

thirty-year-old machinery to make wood-fiber rugs. Woodnotes is now a successful company that exports the majority of its products. It produces blinds, rugs, furniture, room dividers, placemats, table runners, and a collection of handbags—all crafted from humble wood fiber.

When Mikko Puotila, together with his girlfriend and newborn baby son, moved into a building in Espoo, near Helsinki, they called on interior architect Ulla Koskinen for advice. Although the building, which dated from 1981, was designed by the well-known architects Gullichsen-Kairamo-Vormala, the floor plan of their new apartment needed a radical rethink. The space consisted of several small rooms and a long,

Mikko Puotila has furnished his home with Scandinavian design classics and a selection of pieces from Woodnotes.

this page **A room with a view**—the bathroom looks out over the Baltic Sea. The tub is paneled with wenge wood, and the sleek Vola faucet is by Arne Jacobsen. The floor and walls are covered in marble tiles, and a sandblasted glass screen acts as a room divider.

right Like so many Finnish homes, this one has its own sauna. More than just a hot room for cleansing the body, the sauna is used for relaxation and social gatherings, with cold drinks close at hand.

narrow kitchen. Mikko Puotila wanted to transform it into an open space generously lit with natural daylight and with uninterrupted views of the sea.

Ulla Koskinen came up with the idea of relocating the kitchen in a former bedroom with a connecting bathroom, which meant that the existing plumbing could be utilized. Instead of positioning the kitchen work surfaces against an outside wall, the kitchen was opened up toward the living room. The wall between two small bedrooms was removed to create one large master bedroom. All the internal doors were replaced or simply removed, and some of the doorways were widened to increase the feeling of space. Baseboards were removed before an oiled oak floor was laid. Puotila's young son now has plenty of uninterrupted floor space to play and crawl on.

All the internal doors were replaced or removed, and some of the doorways were widened to increase the feeling of space. Baseboards were removed before an oiled oak floor was laid.

Mikko Puotila has furnished his home with a number of Scandinavian design classics, including Arne Jacobsen's Series 7 chairs and Vola faucets, and an Eero Saarinen table, teamed with several modern Italian designs and a selection of pieces from Woodnotes, including oversized floor cushions, rugs, and seating cubes. The only Woodnotes products used sparingly are their blinds—the views of the Baltic Sea outside are just too good to hide.

Finn Juhl and Hanne Wilhelm Hansen

Legendary Danish architect and designer Finn Juhl designed his home in the 1940s, sharing it with Hanne Wilhelm Hansen from 1960. The house is an enduring testament to their shared design philosophy.

The house is filled with many of Juhl's most famous pieces, set against whitewashed wooden floors and plain white walls. The simplicity of the backdrop provides a dramatic contrast with classic Juhl designs such as the Chieftain chair. Ceramics, wooden bowls, and glass objects are dotted around the house, most of which were designed by Juhl. The bookshelves and cupboards were custommade, and most of the lighting is by Juhl. Even the rugs are by Finn Juhl. While Juhl designed the building and most of the objects inside it, Hansen chose much of the artwork.

Born in Copenhagen in 1912, Juhl studied architecture at the Royal Academy of Fine Arts before starting to work for the architect Wilhelm Lauritzen. Between 1935 and 1945, Juhl assisted Lauritzen with his designs for Copenhagen Airport and the Danish

opposite Juhl's 45 Chairs in front of the table were produced by Niels Vodder in 1945. The armchairs on either side were designed in 1944, and only 12 copies were ever made. The wooden bowl was designed by Juhl in 1951 and produced by master turner Magne Monsen.

this page The home office is fitted with custommade bookshelves. Above the desk hangs a lighting pendant designed by Wilhelm Lauritzen for the Danish Broadcasting Corporation building.

Broadcasting Corporation building, two of the most important building projects in Denmark at that time.

After the war, Juhl established his own design practice and became an increasingly important name in Scandinavian design. He was responsible for the interiors of the Georg Jensen stores in New York, Toronto, and London, and the interiors of over thirty Scandinavian Airlines System (SAS) ticket offices around the world. He designed the interior of the Danish ambassador's residence in Washington and the Trusteeship Council Chamber in the UN headquarters in New York.

opposite The Chieftain chair of 1949 is perhaps the best-known of all Juhl's designs. Its distinctive form was directly influenced by African shields.

this page Above the Poet sofa of 1941 hangs a portrait of Hanne Wilhelm Hansen aged 17, painted by Vilhelm Lundstrøm, a good friend of Juhl's, whose work he often used in his interiors. On the floor lies Juhl's Domino rug.

At the same time, Juhl was constantly pouring out designs for furniture, lighting, and other pieces, many of which were used in his interiors. His style was radically different from that of other furniture designers of the time and at the start of his career was considered positively controversial. His inspiration came as much from modern art and abstract shapes as it did from modernist thinking. African arts and craft, together with historical Japanese, Chinese, and Egyptian furniture, were all important influences.

Beech is the wood used for most Danish furniture because it is easy to work with and readily available and therefore inexpensive. Juhl chose to experiment with more exotic woods such as maple, cherry, cedar, palisander, walnut, and even teak, normally only used for outdoor furniture. For over twenty years, Juhl collaborated with the Danish master cabinetmaker Niels Vodder. They developed new methods of joining and bending wood and combining it with leather,

above right The colored cabinet is part of a storage system designed by Juhl in 1974. Only a few were ever made. This was one of Juhl's last designs, but it still looks distinctly modern today.

left This sofa was first shown at the Cabinetmakers Guild in Copenhagen in 1948. It is made from maple and Cuban mahogany with cowhide. The matching armchair was later produced by Baker Furniture in the U.S. By the window on the left stands a small table designed by Nanna Ditzel.

African arts and craft, together with historical Japanese, Chinese and Egyptian furniture, were all important influences.

cane, and upholstery in a decorative fashion. The results were beautiful, but hardly suitable for mass production. Today, Finn Juhl designs produced by Niels Vodder are among the most collectible of all Danish mid-20th-century furniture designs. Two other Danish companies – France & Son and Bovirke – also produced Juhl's furniture. From 1950, Finn Juhl furniture was produced in the U.S. by Baker Furniture. Juhl even designed the company's showroom in Grand Rapids.

Finn Juhl died in 1989, but his reputation is growing rather than fading. With the cooperation of his partner, Hanne Wilhelm Hansen, Finn Juhl furniture is once again being made in Denmark, while their home remains a testament to the talent and energy of an exceptional designer and an exceptional couple.

left Sanaksenaho's home blends into its surroundings like a birdwatcher's hide.

above Finnish pines surround the Finnish-pine façade. The wood was heat-treated to make sure it was perfectly dry and provides good insulation against bad weather.

far right The flat roof is tilted just enough to prevent snow from building up during the winter. The curved front makes reference to Aalto's Finlandia Hall, but on a domestic scale.

Matti Sanaksenaho

The forest home of architect Matti Sanaksenaho is an example of the very best of modern Finnish architecture. Designed to bring the forest outside into the interior, the house is totally integrated into the surrounding landscape.

Even though the home of architect Matti Sanaksenaho is only a modest 1,600 square feet in size, there is nothing modest about Sanaksenaho's professional achievements. He was the man behind the highly acclaimed wood-sided Finnish pavilion at the World Exhibition in Seville in 1992 and was also responsible for creating the flagship store on the Esplanade in Helsinki for Designor, the company that owns Iittala, maker of the Aalto vases. Sanaksenaho also designed the Designor shop in Stockholm. Anyone who has seen these two stores would immediately recognize their similarities with Sanaksenaho's home, but this is not surprising, since Designor's brief was to make the stores look as though someone lived there.

Sanaksenaho's home is located in Espoo, not far from Helsinki, but far enough away to enjoy a real forest surrounding and a view over nearby lakes.

The house was completed in 2002 and took about a year to build. The exterior is completely covered with Finnish pine, which was first heat-treated to make sure it was completely dry and proof against any later warping or shrinkage. Pine is a good insulator that provides suitable protection against changing weather conditions, be they extreme heat or cold. Inside, the floor, parts of the ceiling, and the gallery are crafted from birch, the classic Finnish

Matti Sanaksenaho lives in the house with his family and has a small studio upstairs. The concept was not to build a grand mansion, but to create a family home completely integrated with the surrounding landscape. A terrace and a balcony add to the sense of space, while the large windows and expanses of glass bring the landscape inside. On warm days, meals and social gatherings are enjoyed outside.

above Triple glazing is now standard in most Finnish buildings, and makes building with large areas of glass perfectly viable, despite the cold winters.

right In the evening, the fireplace is the focus of the living room. It also helps to heat the house during the long, cold Finnish winter.

right The ceiling and gallery are covered with birch wood, the wood Alvar Aalto favored for his furniture. In front of the bar stand two model K 65 kitchen stools designed by Aalto for Artek in 1933–35. The open-plan kitchen leads straight into the living area. Behind the curtain is a double door opening onto a large terrace, allowing summer meals to be enjoyed alfresco.

wood, which also appears in the form of the birch furniture used throughout Sanaksenaho's home. The house has triple glazing throughout—a standard Finnish domestic feature, along with having a sauna in the basement (another feature of this house). A heating system has been built into the ceiling of the 23-foot-high living room to project warmth downward, and there are radiators built into the floor just inside the large windows. This very effective heating system has been teamed with a large fireplace for visual warmth and interest.

Sanaksenaho's home makes obvious references to the work of Alvar Aalto, but then Aalto himself was greatly influenced by the Finnish landscape, so it is

The curved façade of Sanaksenaho's house is certainly reminiscent of Finlandia Hall, Alvar Aalto's last large-scale building project in Helsinki.

unsurprising that anyone building a house in a Finnish forest would somehow refer to Aalto's organic style. The curved façade of Sanaksenaho's house is certainly reminiscent of Finlandia Hall, Aalto's last large-scale building project in Helsinki.

Sanaksenaho's house is very representative of modern Finnish architecture. It expresses a desire to bring the landscape indoors and to be close to nature, to enjoy plenty of natural daylight yet be able to gather around an warm fire on dark winter nights. These needs and yearnings are deeply rooted in the Finnish psyche and hold the key to the beauty and integrity of Finnish architecture and design.

left The total ceiling height of the living room is an impressive seven metres. In front of the birch-clad gallery hangs a PH 5 light by Poul Henningsen.

this page Upstairs is a work area with a view of the forest. The chair is a model 68 by Alvar Aalto, designed in 1933–35 and upholstered with a zebra-patterned fabric also designed by Aalto.

Børge and Alice Mogensen's home was built in 1958 and was designed by Børge Mogensen himself. He created his home in much the same way that he created his famous furniture, starting by first considering its function and construction. The house has a passing resemblance to a *finca*—a traditional Spanish farmhouse. There is also a parallel between the appearance of the furniture and the house it sits in; nothing is hidden, nothing is concealed. The oak floor boards were whitewashed and left to age naturally, as was the beech paneled ceiling. The brick walls have been whitewashed to stop the bricks from dusting, but the brickwork is still clearly visible. Parts of the house have tiled floors, but few rugs are laid to soften the lines. Most windows are free of blinds or curtains.

Mogensen's design ethos was political yet practical. His thinking was similar to that of the lighting designer Poul Henningsen, who wanted to create goods that would benefit the masses. In contrast to designers like Finn Juhl, who saw each chair as an individual piece of art, the furniture Mogensen designed was always intended for mass production, albeit a very Danish type of high-quality mass production. One of Mogensen's closest friends was designer Hans Wegner, and their furniture shares a sense of eagerness to honestly reveal every last joint and plug of the construction.

opposite **Beside the fireplace sits a 1962 Conference easy chair in teak. Behind is a Boligens Byggeskape wall unit from 1952, designed by Børge Mogensen and Grethe Meyer.**

above right **A dining chair designed in 1951 sits in front of the oak Shaker table.**

Børge and Alice Mogensen

Børge Mogensen's work could never be described as lighthearted or flirtatious, but his own home shows that his furniture can be both elegant and casual at the same time. It is very Danish, but also very international, drawing on influences from Spain, China, and America.

left **Børge Mogensen designed this sofa, model 2213, for his own home. It went on to become his bestselling sofa and can be seen in Danish embassies around the world. The coffee table is another Mogensen classic dating from 1962. In front sit two Spanish chairs in oak with leather seats, designed in 1959. The chair is Mogensen's Danish adaptation of a traditional Spanish design. They work particularly well in his house, which makes strong references to Mediterranean architecture.**

Børge Mogensen was one of many famous Danish designers who studied under Kaare Klint at the furniture faculty at the Royal Academy of Fine Arts. Klint's teachings included proportional studies to assess the interaction between humans and furniture, and the historical development of furniture. It is thanks to Kaare Klint that a generation of Danish designers was inspired and influenced by Chinese, Spanish, Egyptian, English, and American furniture designs. After completing his studies in 1941, Mogensen worked as an assistant to Klint before he took on

above left **A dividing wall that stops just short of the slanting ceiling divides the kitchen from the dining area. The Shaker table and chairs were designed by Børge Mogensen in 1944 for the Danish Consumer Co-operative, where Mogensen was head of furniture design between 1942 and 1950. The chair is considered a landmark in Danish furniture design.**

above right **The sharply sloping ceilings of the house create dramatic angles and unexpected perspectives.**

the position of head of furniture design at the Danish Consumer Cooperative. His work at the Coop included furniture lines for young children sold under names like Peter's Room and Hansen's Attic. He is also credited with ending the Danish weakness for fake mahogany by introducing beech and oak.

In 1952 Mogensen, in collaboration with Grethe Meyer, created a modular shelving and storage system called Boligens Byggeskape. Mogensen thoroughly researched standard measures for objects like china and shoes, and how many of each the average person owned. With this information he established the optimum size of drawers and shelves and published manuals on storage systems. Between 1955 and 1967 he developed the Øresund series, which took on the gargantuan task of resolving every storage problem in a home. The Øresund series is still produced by Karl Andersson & Söner in Sweden.

By the end of the 1950s, Mogensen's designs were slowly edging toward a purer form of functionalism that was quite unusual at the time. His furniture

below **The Hunting chair was designed in 1950 for the annual Danish Cabinetmakers Guild Exhibition.**

right **Sofa model 1789 was designed by Mogensen in 1945 and is made by Fritz Hansen. Like most upholstered Mogensen furniture, it is covered with fabric designed by Lis Ahlmann.**

opposite **Poul Henningsen's PH 5 lamp is a common feature in Danish homes.**

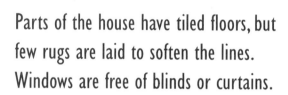

Parts of the house have tiled floors, but few rugs are laid to soften the lines. Windows are free of blinds or curtains.

designs became increasingly pared-down, severe and square, and were less inspired by historical references. However, during the 1960s and 1970s, Mogensen's more austere style became a standard for Danish design. Without having to compromise on his design ethos, Mogensen's furniture grew increasingly popular with upper-middle-class Danes and with official and corporate Denmark, and has remained so to this day. Børge and Alice Mogensen's home serves as a reminder of the many different facets of his work and of his journey from Danish Modern to simply modern.

Many of the objects in Michael Asplund's home only enjoy design-classic status due to the efforts of Michael and his brother Thomas. Through their joint company, simply called Asplund, which they founded in the late 1980s, the Asplunds manufacture and retail modern design. The emphasis is on Sweden and Italy, but they work with international designers from all over the world. As a consequence of his work, almost all the objects in his home are designed by people Michael Asplund knows personally, and are either from the Asplund collection or are sourced from Italy for the Asplund store in central Stockholm.

Rugs and textiles are an important part of the Asplund collection, and important international designers such as Jasper Morrison, Tom Dixon, and Marc Newson have contributed designs. The well-known Swedish architect and designer Thomas Sandell

Michael Asplund

The Stockholm home of furniture manufacturer and retailer Michael Asplund is filled with pieces that reveal the radical shift in Swedish design over the last decade; distinctly Swedish, but with an injection of Italian style.

above **A small wooden Dala horse sits on the coffee table, a symbol of traditional Swedish crafts. The O rug is by Matz Borgström for Asplund.**

right **Wedding stools by Thomas Sandell for Asplund are a modern take on traditional farmhouse furniture. On top are two mugs by Alfredo Häberli for Rörstrand.**

produces designs for Asplund, and there are several pieces of his furniture in the apartment. The Snow series of cabinets by Sandell and fellow Swedish designer Jonas Bohlin is one of the most successful Asplund products, and they appear throughout the apartment in the form of bookshelves, bedside tables, and storage units. The cutout design of their handles is reminiscent of a smiling mouth and bring a spontaneity and humor to the interior.

this page The Italian sofa
and table are flanked by
Alvar Aalto stools and
a Crux rug by Pia Wallén
for Asplund. Like many
Stockholm apartments
dating from the first half
of the 20th century, this
one has a hand-laid
parquet floor, which has
been restored to its
original beauty.

opposite Chairs by Thomas Sandell for Asplund surround the dining table. Behind are shelves displaying glass designs by Ann Wåhlström, Gunnel Sahlin, Ingegerd Råman, and Tom Dixon. The hanging lamp is by Jonas Bohlin.

this page These Slowfox vases by Ingegerd Råman for Orrefors are decorated with a thin, hand-held sandblasting pen, making every vase slightly different to the next.

The Asplund brothers have been particularly active in the revival of Swedish glass design, often staging exhibitions and commissioning special pieces for their store. The apartment contains a selection of the glass Asplund has promoted, including vases by Gunnel Sahlin and Ann Wåhlström for Kosta Boda and by Ingegerd Råman for Orrefors, the two most prominent Swedish glassworks. Another Swedish designer with close links to Asplund is Pia Wallén, and her wool rugs, throws, slippers, and cushions can be found throughout Michael Asplund's home.

There is a serenity and calm to the interior that makes it easy on the eye, yet the decor is far removed

While white is the dominant color in the apartment, textiles and wood bring warmth and life to the interior.

from stark minimalism. While white is the dominant color, textiles and wood bring warmth and life to the interior. The parquet floor is original, as is the open fireplace, which is regularly used during the winter months. Asplund has been a keen follower of the Swedish and international modern art scene for many years, and his home is decorated with a selection of framed artworks and photography.

The housing stock in central Stockholm tends to be quite consistent in style, as most housing was either built during the economic boom of 1890–1910 or between 1935 and 1955, when housing associations first came into existence. Housing development was geographically limited due to the city's location on a group of islands, with the more recently built suburbs set apart from the city center. Functionalist houses from the 1930s on are increasingly popular, because they were well built and planned, and have period details that younger generations now appreciate. Door handles are often made in wood, windows are large, and communal staircases tend to be crafted from marble or local stone. Balconies are standard in both small and larger apartments. Asplund has used the original features of his home to great advantage, and the contemporary furnishings only underline the building's heritage.

Outside, a large balcony overlooks Södermalm, one of the large islands that make up central Stockholm. Traditionally a working-class district, Södermalm is now very popular, due to its pleasant and convivial mix of small shops, bars, and restaurants, which bring people into the neighborhood. Nearby is Mariatorget, a tree-lined square with fountains that is a regular venue for improvised boule tournaments during the summer months.

opposite A row of cabinets designed by Jonas Bohlin and Thomas Sandell for the Asplund furniture collection, offer plenty of practical storage space, while the distinct cut-out "handles" bring a smile to the room.

right In the main bedroom, the bed is covered with a Crux felt throw by Pia Wallén. Hand-woven in southern Sweden from wool collected from local animals, these throws have a weight and density that machine-made throws cannot match, and have become something of an icon of modern Swedish design.

There is a serenity and calm in the interior that makes it easy on the eye and far removed from stark minimalism. Most of the furniture and accessories are either from Asplund's own collection or are sourced from Italy for his Asplund store.

Poul and Hanne Kjærholm

Just north of Copenhagen, along the coastline that overlooks Sweden and the Øresund strait, is a well-kept neighborhood dotted with a string of villas built by some of the greatest names in Danish architecture.

Villa Kjærholm might not be the largest, but it is certainly one of the best-planned buildings in the area. It is also a perfect backdrop for the furniture Poul Kjærholm designed during his 30-year career. The house itself was designed in 1962 by his wife, Hanne Kjærholm, an architect and professor at the Art Academy. Poul Kjærholm died in 1980, but Hanne Kjærholm still lives in the building today, and little has been changed since the house was built.

The most striking feature of the house is the proximity of the waterfront only a few steps outside and the uninterrupted views of the ever-changing scenery. Inside, wooden ceiling beams contrast with the whitewashed walls and the huge glass windows overlooking the water. The house is furnished with many of Kjærholm's own designs, which have developed a rich patina that proves how well modern design can age. The intransigent attitude of Kjærholm's designs remains impressive today: his furniture makes no compromises in terms of quality or function.

Kjærholm was taught both by the designer Hans Wegner and by Jørn Utzon—the architect responsible for Sydney Opera House—at the Art College in Copenhagen in the late 1940s. After leaving college, he worked for Wegner and then for Utzon. In 1955 he embarked upon what was to be

above **The PK 24** *chaise-longue* in woven wicker sits on a delicate stainless-steel frame. The seat angle can be easily adjusted, while the tubular leather headrest cushion is held in place with a weight.

opposite **The black PK 0** chair in molded wood is one of the few Kjærholm designs that does not use steel. Never put into mass production, it is a sculpture as much as a chair. In front of the PK 31/2 leather sofa stands a PK 61 table with a glass top and steel legs. Kjærholm designed the wooden screen on the right especially for the house.

left The screen was designed especially for the house.

above A light fixture by architect Wilhelm Lauritzen.

right Around a PK 54 table sit several PK 9 chairs. Above the table hangs a PH Cascade lamp. Like many Danish designers, Kjærholm used Poul Henningsen's PH light fixtures for Louis Poulsen.

Pieces like the PK 54 have a high level of engineering to them, because Kjærholm avoided obvious design solutions without making the end result look contrived or overdesigned.

his most important collaboration, with the manufacturer Ejvind Kold Christensen. Together they developed some of the most striking and unusual furniture to come out of Scandinavia during this period. Despite his work with the great craftsman Hans Wegner and the prevailing trends of the time, Kjærholm's furniture is based around hard, unyielding materials such as steel, glass, marble, and slate. Although they were designed during the 1950s and 1960s, his pieces have a timeless integrity that means they still look fresh and modern today.

Villa Kjærholm contains examples of the best of Kjærholm's designs. The PK 54 dining table consists of a large, round, flint-rolled slab of marble set upon a satin-brushed stainless-steel frame. Six solid maple leaves slot in around the marble center,

opposite A PK 11 chair from 1957 sits in front of the desk. To the left stands an Oregon pine sideboard by Mogens Koch.

left The PK 1 chair is unusual among Kjærholm's chairs in that it was manufacturered by PP Møbler rather than Ejvind Kold Christensen.

right An Alvar Aalto bar stool stands in the kitchen.

The house is furnished with many of Kjærholm's own designs, which have developed a rich patina that proves how well modern design can age.

increasing the size of the table to over six feet in diameter. The leaves can be stored in a floor-standing rack like a giant set of playing cards or a Japanese sculpture. Pieces like the PK 54 have a high level of engineering to them, because Kjærholm avoided obvious design solutions without making the end result look contrived or overdesigned.

Today, the manufacturer Fritz Hansen has taken over the production of Kjærholm's furniture designs, but his widow, Hanne Kjærholm, still oversees production to make sure that nothing is altered. Not even the palette of leather colors Poul Kjærholm chose for his designs can be changed. It is easy to respect this faithfulness to Kjærholm's memory; his work was based on a precise attention to detail, and it is a heritage worth upholding.

this page The fireplace is so large that it houses the Bang & Olufsen television and the hi-fi system as well as a bookshelf, and also functions as a room divider. A Flexform sofa is positioned behind a coffee table by Hans Wegner. The original parquet flooring has been renovated and is a work of art in itself. To the left is the dining area, which leads to the open-plan kitchen.

opposite The color scheme is kept strictly neutral, with furniture in gray and beige set against white walls. Modern and ultramodern Danish design sits happily alongside each other in the living room.

Sven Markelius was one of the most innovative Swedish architects of the 20th century. He was one of the first to work with concrete back in the 1920s, and his buildings can be found all over Stockholm.

As City Architect during the 1950s and 1960s, Markelius was partly responsible for the complete destruction of some 160 buildings in the heart of Stockholm, some of them dating back to the 17th century. The bold new city grid destroyed the narrow and cramped old street plan, and replaced it with wide, car-friendly thoroughfares lined with parking lots and office buildings. This chapter in Stockholm's architectural history is something many inhabitants look back upon with great indignation, not least because most of the new buildings that replaced the old were not designed by Markelius and are of poor architectural quality. It could be argued that Markelius was a better architect than City Architect; his own buildings are held in much higher esteem than the city plan he implemented.

One such Markelius building is the one where Christer Wallensteen lives with his two young daughters. When Wallensteen found the apartment, it had been used as an office for many years, despite the fact that the rest of the building is given over to residential use. Seven small rooms have been converted into three large, spacious ones, together

Christer Wallensteen

In a 1961 Sven Markelius building in central Stockholm, Christer Wallensteen has transformed a cramped and outdated office space into an airy home for himself and his two daughters. Modern classics and junk-shop finds are mixed with a selection of contemporary pieces.

The interior remains true to its functionalist heritage, retaining the original marble windowsills and beautiful parquet flooring.

with an open-plan living room and kitchen. The interior remains true to its functionalist heritage, retaining the original marble windowsills and beautiful parquet flooring. Wallensteen also retained a dividing wall inset with rippled glass, very Sixties in style but entirely modern in spirit. His greatest triumph was to discover that the huge ventilation pipe that projected through his planned living space could be converted into an massive open fireplace. It is so large that it holds the TV, hi-fi system, and built-in bookshelves, as well as functioning as a room divider.

Christer Wallensteen has furnished the space with neutral pieces in pale colors together with some recognizable modern classics such as the Le Corbusier *chaise-longue* and the Hans Wegner CH 25 wicker chair. Other pieces include secondhand treasures like a plastic string chair dating from the 1950s and a coffee table by Wegner. The ceilings have spotlights set into small brushed-steel boxes, made by the Belgian company Modular and offering an alternative

right **In the foreground stands a CH 25 chair by Hans Wegner, designed in 1951 for Carl Hansen & Søn in Denmark. When Christer Wallensteen renovated the Haga Terminal building, he used dozens of Wegner chairs. On the wall are assorted posters and portraits of family and friends.**

opposite **The rippled glass internal window is part of the original interior by Sven Markelius, dating back to 1961. In front is a quirky and colorful secondhand chair dating from the 1950s and in the background is a Le Corbusier *chaise-longue* covered in pony skin.**

this page The open-plan
kitchen is built from the
Unoform system, designed by
Danish architect Arne Munch
in 1968. The long dining table
with inbuilt candle holders was
designed by Camilla Wessman.
The spotlights, which are set
into small brushed-steel boxes,
are manufactured by the
Belgian company Modular.

to recessed spotlights. The doors in the apartment have rounded windows reminiscent of 1950s' elevator doors, and were designed by Wallensteen himself. The bathroom and kitchen feature Danish design classics such as the Vola series by Arne Jacobsen, the D-line series by Knud Holscher, and the Unoform modular kitchen system, designed by Arne Munch in 1968.

In the course of his work as an interior architect, Christer Wallensteen was responsible for overseeing the renovation of a Danish classic: the 1962 SAS (Scandinavian Airlines System) Haga Terminal building by Hack Kampmann. Originally planned as the first part of a new SAS headquarters, the small building

left **Most doors in the apartment have rounded windows reminiscent of 1950s' elevator doors and were designed by Wallensteen. The chair with plastic string back is a cherished junk-shop find.**

above **Mosaic tiles and oak cabinets set the tone for the bathroom. The extra-long Vola faucet was specially ordered so that it can be swiveled to fill both basin and bathtub.**

is situated in the Haga royal park on the outskirts of Stockholm. It was used as a bus terminal and ticket office before being abandoned. The building had been empty for many years when Wallensteen was asked to renovate it. The Haga Terminal is now a restaurant and conference center with an interior that sensitively respects the original structure while adding modern features. The same description could also be applied to Christer Wallensteen's own home.

below Surrounded by tall pine trees and with dense vegetation growing right up to the the house, the building is at one with nature.

right Aarnio designed the Screw table in 1991 to look like a prop from a film where scientists have shrunk human beings to a fraction of their normal size. Playing with scale is very typical of his work.

Eero Aarnio

The Finnish designer Eero Aarnio is something of a maverick in the design community, but one regarded with great international respect. Aarnio's home reflects his personal design vision, but is also typical of an intellectual outlook on interiors that was particularly prevalent in Finland in the late 1960s.

Eero Aarnio has managed to put his trademark on both pure white and a spectrum of vibrant tones, drawing his design palette from all the colors of the rainbow. Aarnio's own home, in the countryside at Veikkola, outside Helsinki, reflects his personal taste and is a showcase for his designs, but the interior is also very characteristic of a more intellectual approach to interiors that gained popularity in Finland in the late 1960s.

For many, the late 1960s were all about bold colors and groovy psychedelic patterns, but another movement was headed in the opposite direction. After John Lennon met Yoko Ono and became involved with the experimental art scene, the two of them set up home in an all-white house, complete

This page **Two Bubble chairs float like soap bubbles. The see-through design is a reduction of Aarnio's original Ball chair. The chair is suspended from the ceiling to allow Aarnio to dispose of the base, something he wanted to achieve for esthetic reasons. In the background is the Pastil chair, made from two fiberglass halves joined together.**

with white grand piano, white furniture, and white walls. This shift from bold color toward the purity of white is an often-forgotten side of the late 1960s, but at the time it was a refreshing and very radical contrast. The similarity with art gallery interiors is obvious, and the effect is to make the furniture look like part of an installation. This all-white style suited Finland particularly well, because Finnish design has always been reduced in form, and the use of white has been a recurring theme since the work of Alvar Aalto.

During the 1960s and 1970s, together with fellow Finns like Ristomatti Ratia, Yrjö Kukkapuro, and Aarno Ruusuvuori, Aarnio introduced a new sense of modernity and sophistication into Finnish design and brought it to an international audience. Aarnio's designs reveal his preoccupation with new materials and abstract rounded forms. The space-age Ball chair (1966) is a glossy sphere of molded fiberglass that swivels on a steel base, while the Pastil is a curvaceous, abstract update of the rocking chair.

Aarnio's house is filled with prototypes, miniatures, and different versions of his designs, including the celebrated Ball, Pony, and Pastil chairs, showing that while many of his pieces are playful and quirky,

below left Blinds are an effective way of dividing the open floor plan without compromising the airy feel of the interior. The picture on the wall shows an outline of Aarnio's Pony chair.

opposite A wall of bookshelves contrasts with the purity of the interior and shows that the house is a living home. Behind the Ball chair stands a row of miniatures of the chair, manufactured by the Vitra Design company. The Ball chair is a favorite prop for music-video and film producers.

The house is filled with prototypes of Aarnio's own furniture, showing that while many of his pieces are playful and quirky, they also work well in a sophisticated interior.

they also work well in a more sophisticated interior, where their bold, abstract forms operate as sculpture just as much as furniture. The rigid molded fiberglass forms of classic Aarnio pieces such as the Pastil chair may not look inviting at first glance, but its gentle curves cradle a seated body in a comforting fashion. Aarnio's designs provoke an immediate response— few people are able to remain indifferent to them. Their bold and curvy shapes, sly sense of humor, and fantastical forms appeal to both young and old alike. With its strong visual impact, Aarnio's furniture has become something of a must-have for films, music videos, and fashion shoots. The one thing it does require is space, but as Aarnio demonstrates in his own home, many of his pieces can still fit in next to a regular sofa.

this page and opposite
above The living room is
washed with light from the
huge windows. The glass
coffee table is like an
invisible shelf suspended in
midair. The rocking chair
(right) is one of Aarnio's
most recent designs. The
use of tubular steel is
reminiscent of Bauhaus
designs, but the chair has
a playful appeal that is
distinctively Aarnio.

below left and right
Glass sculptures by Aarnio (left) and a glass lamp by Yki Nummi (right) are placed next to miniatures of the Pastil chair, which, just like the full-scale version, float if thrown into water.

Due to the floor-to-ceiling glass windows, Aarnio's home is flooded with natural light all year round. When snow falls in winter and covers the vegetation outside in a thick blanket of white, it underlines the purity and simplicity of the interior. It might seem surprising that Aarnio used so much glass in the construction of his house, since he lives in a country that is covered by snow for at least a quarter of the year. Glass is not a good insulator of heat, but double glazing has been standard for generations in all Nordic countries, and many houses now have triple glazing. It keeps houses warm and snug, and eliminates outside noise, although this is not a problem in the quiet location of the Aarnio house.

If any engine sounds are heard in the house, it is because Aarnio is a Formula 1 fan and watches races on television, following the fortunes of Finnish driver

right **The warm and welcoming kitchen is at the heart of the house. Although open plan, it still retains elements of the traditional farmhouse kitchen, where friends and family gather around. Utensils, pots, and pans are accessible from the practical open shelves.**

Aarnio is a Formula 1 fan and watches races on television, following the fortunes of Finnish driver Mika Häkkinen. His interest in Formula 1 was the inspiration for one of the most recent designs in the house, the Formula chair of 1998.

Mika Häkkinen. His interest in Formula 1 was the inspiration for one of his most recent designs: the Formula chair, which was put into production in 1998. This is a updated version of Aarnio's classic molded fiberglass Pastil chair of 1968, but with a distinctive low-slung sports-car seat shape and a holder for a glass or beer can. The design is proof that Aarnio has a sense of humor, but also a longevity in his design vision, despite changing trends. His house is a perfect testament to this vision.

When Antti and Vuokko Nurmesniemi designed and built their combined home and studio in 1975, they had already been married for 22 years. Quite independently of each other, they have been at the very forefront of Finnish design during the whole second half of the 20th century.

Vuokko Nurmesniemi (née Eskolin) studied at the School of Applied Art in Helsinki and joined the design studio of ceramics factory Arabia in 1952. She became Artistic Director at Marimekko at the tender age of twenty-three, long before the rest of the world had even heard of the company. At Marimekko she fused her knowledge of product design and functionalist thinking with fashion and came up with the Marimekko concept: easy-to-wear clothing, suitable for mass production, with a minimum of buttons, darts, and other fussy details.

In 1953 she produced her striped Piccolo textile design, later made up into Jokapoika (Every Boy) shirts, which became a standard uniform for American architects in the 1960s and are still in production today. While at Marimekko, she also did a spell as designer at Nuutajärvi glassworks under Kaj Franck before leaving the textile company in 1960. In 1964 Vuokko Nurmesniemi started her own

left The sunken area is a feature Alvar Aalto used in many of his buildings, in particular libraries. Antti and Vuokko Nurmesniemi have employed the same concept, but on a domestic scale. The furniture is all by Antti Nurmesniemi, including the custommade sofa.

Antti and Vuokko Nurmesniemi

When two of the best-known designers in Finland built a home together, the result was always going to be spectacular. He is a product designer, she a textile designer, and together Antti and Vuokko Nurmesniemi have both made their creative mark on their home.

this page The Triennial chair was designed by Antti Nurmesniemi in 1960, but only received its name after winning the Grand Prize at the Milan Triennial in 1964, where Antti and Vuokko Nurmesniemi designed the Finnish stand. The chair is still in production by Piiroinen.

right On the stove stand two coffee pots by Antti Nurmesniemi dating from 1957. The design was commissioned by the Wärtsilä corporation because their large cast-iron factory did not have enough orders from the automobile industry to keep it busy at the time.

opposite Three levels in one room. The handrail is a masterpiece of reduction.

fashion house, Vuokko. Her bold pop-art clothing and international success won her great acclaim at home and abroad, and her designs have been described as "garments in a class with industrial design."

Antti Nurmesniemi has enjoyed an equally long and celebrated career. His design work can be found everywhere in Finland, but his most Finnish product is also one of his earliest: the horseshoe-shaped sauna stool he designed for the Palace Hotel in 1951. It might be difficult to find a use for this beautiful stool outside a sauna, but it is nevertheless a design classic. Antti Nurmesniemi established his own design studio in 1956 and has since gone on to work on products

The Nurmesniemi home functions supremely well as a blueprint of the perfect live/work space, but perhaps this is hardly surprising, given the diverse and many talents of Antti and Vuokko Nurmesniemi.

opposite In the foreground is a Deck Chair 001 and to the right are two Lounge Chairs 004, both of which are by Antti Nurmesniemi with upholstery by Vuokko Nurmesniemi.

right The work area of the house has generous storage cupboards and good lighting, teaming an oversized desk lamp with spotlights attached to the ceiling framework.

as diverse as coffee pots, furniture, graphics, and high-voltage transmission towers. Along with Börje Rajalin, he was chief designer of the Helsinki metro trains. Nurmesniemi has also been responsible for a wide variety of interiors, including the Finnish embassy in India. His designs are at the same time very international and intensely Finnish, close to Italian and French postmodernism, but always infused with Finnish functionality and color. Antti Nurmesniemi has won countless awards and titles, including that of professor and president of the ICSID (International Council of Societies of Industrial Design).

The Nurmesniemi home is the ultimate open-plan interior, thought out long before open-plan homes became a fashion statement. The industrial-looking ceiling framework gives it a distinctive appearance, and the ease with which different levels are combined is impressive. There is a sunken area in the main room that contrasts perfectly with a raised area right next to it, giving a bird's-eye view of three floors stacked in the same space without feeling cramped or crowded. Years ahead of its time, the Nurmesniemi home functions supremely well as a blueprint of the perfect live/work space, but perhaps this is hardly surprising given the diverse and many talents of Antti and Vuokko Nurmesniemi.

left The Hockney sofa is by Eero Koivisto for David Design, and the PK 22 chairs are by Poul Kjærholm. The oak units were designed by Eva Lilja Löwenhielm and Anya Sebton.

right An open staircase is reduced to its bare minimum. The plaster casts are molded from Eva's husband's feet.

Eva Lilja Löwenhielm

A 1966 semi-detached house in a leafy Stockholm suburb has been transformed by the designer Eva Lilja Löwenhielm to suit both her family and her work.

After leaving Beckmans design school in Stockholm in 1996, Eva Lilja Löwenhielm was awarded a scholarship by Swedish *Elle Decoration* and a prize for good new design by the Swedish Design Council. Producing work for both the Swedish furniture giant IKEA and many other smaller manufacturers allows Löwenhielm to vary her creative output. She works in many different materials—glass, wood, textiles, and ceramics—and has created interiors for shops, homes, and hotels. Her style is typical of good Scandinavian design; it is simple, beautiful, and functional with a sense of humor, but it never screams for attention.

Her own home has offered a great opportunity for Eva Lilja Löwenhielm to try out new ideas and to create the right setting for her own designs. Like many semi-detached houses built in Sweden during the 1960s, the structural quality and spacious floor plan were excellent, but attention to detail was somehow lacking when the house was first built. Eva Lilja Löwenhielm has stripped the house of all extraneous details—baseboards, some internal doors, and even the staircase handrail. Where she has replaced items, she has used a simple palette of white, gray, and natural oak. Great attention has been paid to creating good storage facilities, which make it possible to conceal any clutter and mess. With two small children, this might sound like an impossible task, but in fact

The overall impression is that of order and structure, but also comfort and ease of living—a harmonious combination of modern Swedish style and traditional Shaker interiors.

opposite **Wishbone chairs by Hans Wegner sit around the dining table. In front is a child's play area with Alvar Aalto stools.**

left **Behind the dining table is a long sideboard storing china and glass.**

above right **The open-plan kitchen with its sleek white cabinets works well with the rest of the house.**

having fewer items around actually makes life easier—there are simply fewer items to break and there is more space to play in.

Most of the furniture in the house consists of Scandinavian design classics from the middle of the last century—the PK 22 chair by Poul Kjærholm, the Wishbone chair by Hans Wegner, and Ant and 3107 chairs by Arne Jacobsen. Other furniture includes more recent creations, like the Hockney sofa and

daybed by Eero Koivisto for the Swedish furniture company David Design. The floor is covered with large hand-tufted wool rugs designed by Eva Lilja Löwenhielm for the IKEA designer collection PS. The overall impression is one of order and structure, but also comfort and ease of living—a harmonious combination of modern Swedish style and traditional Shaker interiors.

Most of the furniture in the house consists of Scandinavian design classics from the middle of the last century.

above left The Hang Over chair by Finnish designer Vertti Kivi is suspended from the ceiling alongside the staircase. The rug was designed by Eva Lilja Löwenhielm for IKEA.

left The studio has a row of white cabinets that offer generous storage space. Each desk has a classic chair: the Wishbone by Hans Wegner and the 3117 by Arne Jacobsen.

right The bedroom is the simplest room, providing an atmosphere of calm tranquility. The window offers views over the Baltic Sea.

This look has become popular in Sweden in the last few years, with architects like Jonas Lindvall and the trio Claesson Koivisto Rune acting as flagbearers. Eva Lilja Löwenhielm's home achieves this with large expanses of white wall, broken up by doors or openings with a minimal architectural framework. Cables, ducts, and pipes are all concealed, and the oak floor meets the walls without any baseboards. The overall look might appear simple and achievable, but in reality, if you want to create this kind of effect, it is essential to have a contractor who is able to appreciate the importance of the perfect finish.

right In a child's bedroom, a colorful Jungle puzzle designed by Pan Toivanen for Finnish company Artek sits on top of the versatile cube storage unit. The bed is covered by a modern classic: a handwoven Cross throw by Pia Wallén. Only 100 throws are made each year on a wooden loom that dates back to the 19th century. On the floor is a wool rug designed by Eva Lilja Löwenhielm for IKEA.

Resources

The following retailers stock a selection of Scandinavian design, from vintage to modern reissues.

ABC Carpet & Home

881 Broadway and
East 19th Street
New York, NY 10003
(212) 473-3000

www.ABC.com

Visit the store's vintage modern section for twentieth-century Scandinavian rugs, furniture, and accessories.

Abodeon

1731 Massachusetts Avenue
Cambridge, MA 02138
(617) 497-0137

Twentieth-century furniture and accessories, with an emphasis on Scandinavian design.

Antik

104 Franklin Street
New York, NY 10011
(212) 343-0471

Modern Scandinavian glassware, lighting, and furniture, including an extensive selection of ceramics.

Art & Industrial Design

399 Lafayette Street
New York, NY 10003
(212) 477-0116

www.aid20c.com

Inventory includes classic Scandinavian designs, from furniture to glassware.

Baldinger Lighting

19-02 Steinway Street
Astoria, NY 11105
(718) 204-5700

www.baldingerlighting.com

Official U.S. importer of Alvar Aalto and other Artek light fixtures.

B4 20th Century Design

539 East 12th Street
New York, NY 10009
(212) 505-5344

www.b4decor.com

Late modern vintage from an assortment of international designers, including ceramics by Gustavsberg, glass by Orrefors, and chairs by Finnish designer Yrjo Kukkapuro.

Brayton International

Call (212) 445-8915 or visit www.brayton.com for the retail outlet nearest you.

Manufacturer of Finn Juhl and Hans Wegner in the U.S.

Circa50

5777 Main Street
Manchester Center
VT 05255
(802) 362-3796

www.circa50.com

Current productions of modern Scandinavian classics by Knoll, Herman Miller, Vitra, and more.

City Schemes

22 Kent Street
Sommerville, MA 02143
(617) 776-7777

www.cityschemes.com

Contemporary furniture, including modern reissues of Scandinavian classics.

Collage 20th Century Classics

1300 North Industrial
Boulevard
Dallas, TX 75207
(214) 828-9888

www.collageclassics.com

Vintage designer and architect-designed decorative arts, including all the important names in Scandinavian design.

Crate & Barrel

Call (800) 967-6696 or visit www.crateandbarrel.com for retail outlet near you.

Marimekko textiles and Iittala glassware are sold through this large home décor chain.

Design Quest

4181 28th Street SE
Grand Rapids, MI 49512
(800) 944-3232

www.d2d2d2.com

Stocks modern reissues of Scandinavian furniture, including the Fredericia brand.

Design Store

(888)279-0571

www.designstore.com

Online store with a large inventory in modern furniture and tableware, including a selection of Scandinavian manufacturers and designers.

Design Within Reach

455 Jackson Street
San Francisco, CA 94111
(800) 944-2233

www@dwr.com

Although this West Coast firm caters to professionals, the public is welcome in its showrooms, which carries classic designs by Alvar Aalto among others.

Egbert's

2231 First Avenue
Seattle, WA 98121
(206) 728-5682

Modern Scandinavian furniture and tableware.

Gilda's Imports

30 South Clinton Street
Iowa City, IA 52240
(319) 338-7700

Modern reissues of classic Scandinavian furniture as well as tableware, including the Iittala and Rörstrand brands.

Finnish Gifts, Inc.

(800) 866-FINNISH

www.finnishgifts.com

This Minnesota based online store is an authorized retailer of Iittala (including the Arabia, Hackman, and Rorstrand brands) and Artek furniture.

Georg Jensen

683 Madison Avenue
New York, NY 10021
(212) 759-6457

www.georgjenson.com

U.S. headquarters of this Danish metalware company; call or visit the website for a retail outlet near you.

Greg Nanamura

1038 Lexington Avenue
New York, NY 10021
(917)446-4170

www.gregnanamura.com

Scandinavian silver and jewelry are one specialty for this dealer; his showroom is open to the public but you must call ahead to see the jewelry.

Herman Miller Inc.

855 East Main Avenue
Zeeland, MI 49464-0302
(616) 654 3860

www.hermanmiller.com

Official U.S. importer of Artek furniture including, of course, Alvar Aalto designs.

Highbrow Inc.

2110 8th Avenue South
Nashville, TN 37204
(888) 329-0219

www.highbrowfurniture.com

An authorized Herman Miller Knoll, Louis Poulsen, and Vitra dealer that specializes in mid-century decorative arts, including Scandinavian items.

Gilda's Imports

IKEA

Call (800) 434-4532 or visit www.ikea-us.com for your nearest store.

The IKEA PS and A.I.R. collections are worth a look for slightly more cutting-edge designs from this Swedish home furnishings giant.

Iittala

Visit www.iittalafi.com for a retail outlet near you.

Lampa + Möbler

8317 Beverly Boulevard
Los Angeles, CA 90048
(323) 852-1542

www.lampamobler.com

This dealer began as a small lighting showroom, but now sells modern-contemporary Swedish furniture, including Bruno Mathsson, online.

Liten Hus

Mall of America
138 South Boulevard
Bloomington, MN 55245
(952) 858-8256

www.litenhaus.com

Retailer of a wide variety of Scandinavian furniture, rugs, and accessories, modern and contemporary.

Lost City Arts

18 Cooper Square
New York, NY 10003
(212) 375-0500

www.lostcityarts.com

Sells vintage Poul Kjærholm, Børge Mogensen, Verner Panton, Fritz Hansen, Hans Wegner, Arne Jacobsen, and more.

Louis Poulsen Lighting, Inc.

3260 Meridian Parkway
Fort Lauderdale, FL 33331
(954) 349-2525

www.louis-poulsen.com

Contact the U.S. showroom for a retail outlet near you.

Marimekko

Donna Gorman, Inc.
1115 Weed Street
New Canaan, CT 06840
(203) 972-3685

Contact the U. S. showroom for a retail outlet near you.

Michael C. Fina

545 Fifth Avenue
New York, NY 10017
(212) 557-2500
www.michaelcfina.com

Scandinavian silver, crystal, and other tableware.

Michigan Street Antiques & Vintage Modern

1049 East Michigan Street
Indianapolis, IN 46202
(317) 298-9978
www.themodernline.com

Arne Jacobsen, Hans Wegner, and Finn Juhl designs are part of this store's online selection of Scandinavian furniture and lighting. Look here for glass and ceramic pieces, too.

Modern Times

1538 North Milwaukee
Avenue
Chicago, IL 60622
(773) 772-8871
www.moderntimeschicago.com

Mid-century modern furniture, lighting, and accessories, including Scandinavian furniture, glass, and ceramics.

Modhaus

Boston, MA
(617) 822-9183
www.modhaus.com

Online gallery of furnishings and decorative objects from the 1950s to 1970s, including Scandinavian designs and handcrafts. Call ahead to visit the warehouse.

Modlivin

5327 East Colfax Avenue
Denver, CO 80220
(720) 941-9292
www.modlivin.com

Mid-century furniture and accessories, including the work of Eero Aarnio and other Scandinavian designers.

Moss

146 Greene Street
New York, NY 10012
(212) 226-2190
www.mossonline.com

20th-century design, home furnishings, and decorative accessories, including Federicia.

ORAIC Design Corp

275 Grove Street
Suite 2-400
Newton, MA 02466
(888) GO-ORIAC
www.oriac.com

Online catalog for designer furniture and accessories, including Verner Panton designs.

1950

P.O. Box 1206
Pell City, AL 35125
(678) 938-5842
www.1950.com

Scandinavian ceramics and glass are the specialty of this online store, which carries a range of vintage Scandinavian accessories.

ReGeneration Modern Furniture

38 Renwick Street
New York, NY 10013
(212) 741-2102
www.regenerationfurniture.com

Specializes in mid-century vintage furniture with a focus on the 1950s. Danish designers include Poul Kjærholm, Børge Mogensen, and Hans Wegner.

Retromodern.com, Inc.

805 Peachtree Street, NE
Atlanta, GA 30308
(404) 724-0093
www.retromodern.com

Retailer of reissues and current productions of Scandinavian designs by Fritz Hansen, Iittala, Stelton, and more.

R 20th Century Design

82 Franklin Street
New York, NY 10013
(212) 343-7979
www.r20thcentury.com

A comprehensive selection of mid-century modern furniture, lighting, and accessories from a complete list of the important designers and manufacturers, including Arne Jacobsen, Poul Henningsen, Hans and Florence Knoll, Finn Juhl, and Poul Kjærholm. Their "wishlist" service helps you search for a specific piece or designer.

Scandinavian Design Inc.,

347 Fifth Avenue, Suite 10009
New York, NY 10016
(212) 213-0009
www.scandinaviandesigninc.com

For the past 50 years, this dealer (it's open to the public and online) has specialized in modern Scandinavian furniture and lighting, ranging from Louis Poulson and Alvar Aalto lighting to Bruno Mathsson and Fritz Hansen furniture.

Scandia Imports

1286 Soland Avenue
Albany, CA 94706
(510) 525-7370

More than 4,000 items imported from Scandinavian countries, including modern Scandinavian home furnishings and accessories.

Shari Euro Trends

1430 Kurtis Lane
Lake Forest, IL 60045
(847) 735-1557

Eero Aarnio's plastic furniture and other Scandinavian pieces.

The Showplace

40 West 25th Street, Shop 130
New York, NY 10010
(212) 645-3671
www.@jensensilver.com

Georg Jensen designs and the work of other Scandinavian silversmiths and jewelers.

Tabletools

85 Furniture Row
Milford, CT 06460
(888) 211-6603
www.tabletools.com

Online source for design-oriented table, kitchen, and barware, including Stelton, Hackman, Iittala, Rörstrand, and Arabia brands.

The Terence Conran Shop

407 East 59th Street
New York, NY 10022
(212) 755-9079
www.conran.com

Arne Jacobsen and Verner Panton furniture, as well as a selection of Le Klint lamps.

20CDesign.com

4027 Main Street
Dallas, TX 75214
(214) 821-0262
www.20Cdesign.com

Specializes in classic modern design. Scandinavian designers and manufactures include Fritz Hansen, Hans Wegner, Poul Kjærholm, and more.

Textile Arts

P.O. Box 3151
Sag Harbor, New York 11963
(888) 343-7285
www.txtlart.com

Mail-order fabrics shop specializing in Marimekko.

TR Christian

3410 West 70th Street
Galleria, Edina, MN 55435
(952) 925-5278
www.trchristian.com

Glass, silver, and other tableware, including Iittala and other major Scandinavian manufacturers.

2 Danes

73 White Bridge Road
Suite 109
Nashville, TN 37205
(615) 352-6085

Modern reissues of Scandinavian furniture, lighting, rugs, and more.

Unica Home

7540 South Industrial Road,
Suite 501
Las Vegas, NV 89139-5965
(888) 89-UNICA
www.unicahome.com

Carries a wide range of Scandinavian furniture, lighting, ceramics, and other accessories, including the work of George Jensen, Hackman, Iittala, Marimekko, and Arabia.

Vintage Modern Design

35 Keswick Road
South Portland, Maine 04106
(207) 874-7960
www.vintagemoderndesign.com

Offerings from this online store include Scandinavian furniture, lighting, ceramics, and glass.

Vitra Inc.

149 Fifth Avenue
New York, NY 10010
(212) 539-1900
www.vitra.com

Contact the showroom or visit the website to find your nearest retailer of Verner Panton and other Vitra designers.

Architects and designers

Whose work appears in this book:

Eero Aarnio
www.eero-aarnio.com
t. +358 9 25 68 547
Pages 2, 48, 49 r, 118-125

AEM Architects
80 O'Donnell Court
Brunswick Centre
Brunswick Square
London WC1N 1NX
t. +20 7713 9191
f. +20 7713 9199
Pages 50 l, 58-59

Galerie Mikael Andersen
Bredgade 63
DK-1260 Copenhagen
Denmark
t. +45 33 33 05 12
f. +45 33 15 45 93
www.gma.dk
Pages 64-69

Asplund
(Showroom and shop)
Sibyllegatan 31
114 42 Stockholm
Sweden
t. +46 8 662 52 84
Pages 3, 24-25, 33-34 a, 100-104

Avanti Architects Limited
1 Torriano Mews
London NW5 2RZ
t. +20 7284 1616
f. +20 7284 1555
Page 56

Paul Daly Design Studio Ltd
11 Hoxton Square
London N1 6NU
t. +20 7613 4855
f. +20 7613 5848
email: studio@pauldaly.com
www.pauldaly.com
Page 40 b

Nanna Ditzel MDD FCSD
Industrial designer
specializing in furniture,
textiles, jewellery and
exhibitions
Nanna Ditzel Design
Klareboderne 4
DK-1115 Copenhagen K
Denmark
www.nanna-ditzel-design.dk
Pages 50 r, 52-53 l

Echo Design Agency
5 Sebastien Street
London EC1V OHD
t. +20 7251 6990
f. +20 7251 6885
Page 40 b

Johnson Naylor
13 Britton Street
London EC1M 5SX
t. +20 7490 8885
f. +20 7490 0038
email:
brian.johnson@johnsonnaylor.co.uk
Pages 23 r, 40 ac

Finn Juhl Furniture
t. +45 39 63 60 09
att. Hanne Wilhelm Hansen
Pages 8, 9 r, 20 br, 21 a, 38 l, 38 br, 60, 82-87

Kjærholm's
Rungstedvej 86
DK-2960 Rungsted Kyst
Denmark
t. +45 45 76 56 56
f. +45 45 76 76 21
email: info@kjaerholms.dk
www.kjaerholms.dk
Pages 7 main, 21 br-22l, 25 inset, 106-111

Grethe Meyer MAA
Designer and architect
Royal Scandinavia A/S
Smallegade 45
2000 Frederiksberg
Denmark
t. +45 38 14 4848
Pages 20 bl, 38-39ar, 45 b, 70-75

Modernity
Köpmangatan 3
111 31 Stockholm
Sweden
t. +46 8 20 80 25
www.modernity.se
Pages Endpapers, 10, 12-13, 16 a, 16-17, 22-23, 41 r, 59 r

Studio Nurmesniemi/
Antti Nurmesniemi
t. +358 9 6847055
f. +358 9 6848325

Construction: Paloheimo &
Ollila, Engineers
Heating, plumbing, air: Olavi
Pohjalaínen, engineer
Electricity: Risto Mäenpää,
engineer
Pages 36-37, 46 a, 126-131

Ratia Brand Co Oy
Kapteeninkatu 1 E
00140 Helsinki
Finland
t. +358 9 622 72820
f. +358 9 622 72821
m. +358 50 554 4788
email: ratia@ratia.com
www.ratia.com
Pages 4-5, 11, 26-27

Sanaksenaho Architects
Tehtaankatu 13C
00140 Helsinki
t. +358 9 177 341
f. +358 9 630 636
email: arch@sanaks.pp.fi
Pages 14-15, 88-93

Stelton AS
P.O. Box 59
Gl. Vartov Vej 1
DK 2900 Hellerup
Denmark
t. +45 3962 3055
f. +45 3962 2350
email: stelton@stelton.dk
www.stelton.com
Pages 44 inset, 45 a, 47 l, 55, 57, 62-63

Jyrki Tasa, Architect
Nurmela-Raimoranta-Tasa
Architects
Kalevankatu 31
00100 Helsinki
Finland
t. +358 9 6866780
f. +358 9 6857588
m. +358 40 505 7300
email: tasa@n-r-t.fi
www.n-r-t.fi
Pages 6, 15 r, 29 r, 53 r

VX design & architecture
t./f. +20 7370 5496
email: vx@vxdesign.com
www.vxdesign.com
Page 51

Wallensteen & Co ab
Architect and Design
Consultants
Floragatan 11
114 31 Stockholm
Sweden
t./f. +46 8 210151
m. +46 70 7203117
email: wallensteen@chello.se

Lighting:
  Konkret Architects/Gerhard
Rehm
Pages 112-117

Woodnotes OY
Tallberginkatu 1B
00180 Helsinki
Finland
t. +358 9694 2200
f. +358 9694 2221
email: woodnotes@woodnotes.fi
www.woodnotes.fi
Pages 17 c, 17 r, 24 l, 34 b-35, 76-81

Picture credits

Photography by Andrew Wood (unless stated otherwise)

KEY: **a**=above, **b**=below, **r**=right, **l**=left, **c**=center

Endpapers Andrew Duncanson's (owner of Modernity) apartment in Stockholm, Sweden; **1** The Mogensen family's home in Gentofte, Denmark; **2** Eero Aarnio's house in Veikkola, Finland; **3** Michael Asplund's apartment in Stockholm, Sweden; **4-5** Ristomatti Ratia's apartment in Helsinki, Finland; **6** Into Tasa's house in Espoo, Finland, designed by architect Jyrki Tasa; **7 main** The Kjærholms' family home in Rungsted, Denmark; **7 inset** A house in Stockholm, Sweden; **8** & **9 r** The Finn Juhl house, Charlottenlund, Denmark; **9 l** The Mogensen family's home in Gentofte, Denmark; **10** Andrew Duncanson's (owner of Modernity) apartment in Stockholm, Sweden; **11** Ristomatti Ratia's apartment in Helsinki, Finland; **12-13** Andrew Duncanson's (owner of Modernity) apartment in Stockholm, Sweden; **14-15** Matti and Pirjo Sanaksenaho's house in Espoo, Finland, designed by Sanaksenaho Architects; **15 r** Into Tasa's house in Espoo, Finland, designed by architect Jyrki Tasa; **16 a** & **16-17** Andrew Duncanson's (owner of Modernity) apartment in Stockholm, Sweden; **16 b** A house in Stockholm, Sweden; **17 c** & **r** Mikko Puotila's apartment in Espoo, Finland. Interior design by Ulla Koskinen; **18-19** Coexistence, 020 7354 8817; **20 al** The Mogensen family's home in Gentofte, Denmark; **20 bl** Architect Grethe Meyer's house, Hørsholm, Denmark. Built by architects Moldenhawer, Hammer and Frederiksen, 1963; **20 ar** ph Thomas Stewart/Target Gallery, London; **20 br** & **21a** The Finn Juhl house, Charlottenlund, Denmark; **21 bl** ph Thomas Stewart/Ice bucket and wooden bowl courtesy of Origin; **21 br-22 l** The Kjærholms' family home in Rungsted, Denmark; **22-23** Andrew Duncanson's (owner of Modernity) apartment in Stockholm, Sweden; **23 r** Brian Johnson's apartment in London, designed by Johnson Naylor; **24 l** Mikko Puotila's apartment in Espoo, Finland. Interior design by Ulla Koskinen; **24-25** Michael Asplund's apartment in Stockholm, Sweden; **25 inset** The Kjærholms' family home in Rungsted, Denmark; **26-27** Ristomatti Ratia's apartment in Helsinki, Finland; **28-29** & **29 l** ph Thomas Stewart/Target Gallery, London; **29 r** Into Tasa's house in Espoo, Finland, designed by architect Jyrki Tasa; **30 a** ph Thomas Stewart/Target Gallery, London; **30 b** ph Thomas Stewart/Glass courtesy of Skandium; **31** ph Thomas Stewart/Century London 020 7487 5100/Ceramic dishes courtesy of Gary Grant Choice Pieces; **32** & **33 inset** A house in Stockholm, Sweden; **33-34 a** Michael Asplund's apartment in Stockholm, Sweden; **34 b-35** Mikko Puotila's apartment in Espoo, Finland. Interior design by Ulla Koskinen; **36-37** Antti Nurmesniemi's house in Helsinki, Finland; **37 ar** ph Chris Everard/Ben Atfield's house in London; **37 br** ph Thomas Stewart; **38 l** & **38 br** The Finn Juhl house, Charlottenlund, Denmark; **38-39** & **39 ar** Architect Grethe Meyer's house, Hørsholm, Denmark. Built by architects Moldenhawer, Hammer and Frederiksen, 1963; **39 background** ph Tham Nhu-Tran; **40 al** ph Thomas Stewart/Target Gallery, London; **40 ac** ph Tham Nhu-Tran/Brian Johnson's apartment in London, designed by Johnson Naylor; **40 b** ph Thomas Stewart/Yuen-Wei Chew's apartment in London designed by Paul Daly represented by Echo Design Agency/White tableware courtesy of Rosenthal China; **40-41** ph Thomas Stewart/Target Gallery, London; **41 r** Andrew Duncanson's (owner of Modernity) apartment in Stockholm, Sweden; **42 l** ph Thomas Stewart/Century London 020 7487 5100/Dish courtesy of Gary Grant Choice Pieces; **42-43** ph Thomas Stewart/Tableware courtesy of Skandium; **43 r** ph Thomas Stewart/Century London 020 7487 5100; **44** A house in Stockholm, Sweden; **44 inset** & **45 a** Peter Holmblad's apartment in Klampenborg, Denmark, designed by architect Arne Jacobsen in 1958; **45 background** ph Tham Nhu-Tran; **45 b** Architect Grethe Meyer's house, Hørsholm, Denmark. Built by architects Moldenhawer, Hammer and Frederiksen, 1963; **46 a** Antti Nurmesniemi's house in Helsinki, Finland; **47 l** Peter Holmblad's apartment in Klampenborg, Denmark, designed by architect Arne Jacobsen in 1958; **47 r** A house in Stockholm, Sweden; **48** & **49 r** Eero Aarnio's house in Veikkola, Finland; **49 l** ph Thomas Stewart/Bowls courtesy of Skandium; **50 l** ph Chris Everard/a loft apartment in London designed by AEM Architects, lights courtesy of Skandium; **50 r** Nanna Ditzel's home in Copenhagen; **51** Ian Chee's apartment in London, chair courtesy of Vitra; **52-53 l** ph Nanna Ditzel's home in Copenhagen; **53 r** Into Tasa's house in Espoo, Finland, designed by architect Jyrki Tasa; **54 l** ph Chris Everard/Christina Wilson's house in London, lights courtesy of Century; **54 r** The Mogensen family's home in Gentofte, Denmark; **55** Peter Holmblad's apartment in Klampenborg, Denmark, designed by architect Arne Jacobsen in 1958; **56** ph Chris Everard/ Justin de Syllas & Annette Main's house in London, light courtesy of Skandium; **57** Peter Holmblad's apartment in Klampenborg, Denmark, designed by architect Arne Jacobsen in 1958; **58 l** ph Alan Williams/Director of design consultants Graven Images, Janice Kirkpatrick's apartment in Glasgow; **58-59** ph Chris Everard/a loft apartment in London designed by AEM Architects, lights courtesy of Skandium; **59 r** Andrew Duncanson's (owner of Modernity) apartment in Stockholm, Sweden; **60** The Finn Juhl house, Charlottenlund, Denmark; **61** ph Chris Everard/Christina Wilson's house in London; **62-63** Peter Holmblad's apartment in Klampenborg, Denmark, designed by architect Arne Jacobsen in 1958; **64-69** Gallery owner Mikael Andersen's studio house in Denmark, designed by Henning Larsen; **70-75** Architect Grethe Meyer's house, Hørsholm, Denmark. Built by architects Moldenhawer, Hammer and Frederiksen, 1963; **76-81** Mikko Puotila's apartment in Espoo, Finland. Interior design by Ulla Koskinen; **82-87** The Finn Juhl house, Charlottenlund, Denmark; **88-93** Matti and Pirjo Sanaksenaho's house in Espoo, Finland, designed by Sanaksenaho Architects; **94-99** The Mogensen family's home in Gentofte, Denmark; **100-104** Michael Asplund's apartment in Stockholm, Sweden; **106-111** The Kjærholms' family home in Rungsted, Denmark; **112-117** Christer Wallensteen's apartment in Stockholm, Sweden; **118-125** Eero Aarnio's house in Veikkola, Finland; **126-131** Antti Nurmesniemi's house in Helsinki, Finland; **132-137** A house in Stockholm, Sweden.

Index

Page numbers in *italic* refer to captions and illustrations

ACKNOWLEDGMENTS

Magnus Englund and Chrystina Schmidt would like to thank Christopher Seidenfaden for believing in Skandium and thereby making this book possible; all our staff at Skandium and Marimekko in Britain; Kati Horttanainen for her amazing Finnish spelling skills and cool head; the Danish and Finnish embassies in London and the Finnish Architectural Society for location tips; all the location owners for so kindly allowing us to photograph their homes, especially Andrew Duncan at Modernity and Ristomatti Ratia; Artek and Marimekko in Helsinki, and Peter Husted at Stelton for their general help and continuous inspiration. Finally, warm thanks to Britt Englund for the excellent press cutting service.